In Laos and Siam

In Laos and Siam

Marthe Bassenne

Translation and Introduction
by

Walter E. J. Tips

White Lotus
Bangkok   Cheney

In memory of a loyal colleague and companion on the road

Khun Suda
(13 March 1967–9 October 1994)

who died in the line of duty and who belied every bad word
that is said about the Siamese work ethics in this book.

ด้วยความระลึกถึงเพื่อนร่วมงานและเพื่อนร่วมเดินทางที่แสนดี

คุณสุดา

(13 มีนาคม 2510 – 9 ตุลาคม 2537)

ผู้ซึ่งเสียชีวิตในระหว่างปฏิบัติหน้าที่ราชการ

White Lotus Co., Ltd
G.P.O. Box 1141
Bangkok 10501

Originally published as **Au Laos et Au Siam,** 1912, Marthe Bassenne in *Le Tour du Monde*, Vol. 18 N.S., Paris.

Printed in Thailand

Typeset by COMSET Limited Partnership

ISBN 974-8496-29-5   pbk.   White Lotus Co., Ltd.; Bangkok
ISBN 1-879155-45-1   pbk.   White Lotus Co., Ltd.; Cheney

Contents

Introduction

We know very little about the author of this travelogue to Laos and Siam. And little do we want factual information because this was and is a book of impressions and feelings. Mme Marthe Bassenne had earlier published, in *Le Tour du Monde*, an account of her travel to Cochinchina where her husband, Doctor Bassenne, was employed. Like so many French professionals, it is likely that the lure of this relatively peaceful part of French Indochina had set their hearts racing. The trip to their place of work took them overland, across Central Asia. The present original first edition, and perhaps the only edition as no books of Marthe are known, was also published in the French travel magazine *Le Tour du Monde*.

The magazine *Le Tour du Monde* was founded in 1860 under the direction of Édouard Charton and the engravings to illustrate it, were done by 'our most celebrated artists.' The Librarie Hachette et Cie published it from its office in Paris at the Boulevard Saint-Germain and listed its British office on King William Street, at the Strand, on the frontispiece. However, the content was neither germane to the Parisians, nor were most of the regions, cities and countries described on its pages saintly. This was the beginning of an age of the rough and ready explorers, under the patronage of princes, kings and businessmen with an eye on overseas expansion. They went on a rampage to acquire fame, business interests, trading posts, and land...as much territory as possible, for settlers from Europe.

Le Tour du Monde must have been and was until well into the twentieth century, a notable magazine. Not only because it was lavishly illustrated, with engravings first, and by the 1890s also with splendid photographs, but also because famous and infamous explorers published their stories in it. These were often first editions, without the tedium of scientific and business reports, certainly with any 'trade intelligence' prudently removed, but with colorful anecdotes of wild animals, local mystery men, and semi-civilized tribes, since, in that age, no-one questioned the superiority of a Judeo-Christian Western world concept that had not yet been seriously challenged by Darwinism or modern scientific developments. Among the notable accounts were also translations: for example A. R. Wallace's discoveries in the Indo-Malayan world of animals and plants, were 'hot' enough to find their way into *Le Tour du Monde* as books in their first French translation. Stanley's attempts to find Livingstone and the latter's own final hours and decease, as recorded in his diaries, were translated for consumption by the vast number of intellectuals and politicians who mastered French, then still a *lingua franca* and the diplomatic language par excellence, better than English, a trader's parlance.

Often, we no longer remember such first, serialized editions: who would, for example, know that Francis Garnier's account of the mission that had begun with Doudart de Lagrée's exploration of the Mekong, had been published in *Le Tour du Monde*'s editions of the early 1870s. In 1863, volume VIII of the magazine carried the *Voyage dans les Royaumes de Siam, de Cambodge, de Laos et Autres Parties Centrales de l'Indo-Chine* of Henri Mouhot, 'a French naturalist.' Richly illustrated with drawings based on photographs that was each one in itself a masterpiece, even though the magazine was, of course, all black and white.

Thus, do we take all what has been described in these pages in black and white. More so because, like Marthe Bassenne's work, many travelogues were almost copied word-by-word from a carefully conserved and religiously kept up-to-date diary. Even though engravings are often marked as '*d'après M. Mouhot*,' for his work as for most others, we believe, that, in most editions, the artist's creativity has been neatly channeled, if not restrained, by meticulously detailed descriptions of what struck the eye of the Western traveler in these strange worlds of savage rivers and dense jungles. Marthe Bassenne however, writing in 1909, and apparently armed with a camera, was already living in that age of stills, albeit black and white, that leave much less to be filled in by the imagination of the artist. What she did not record herself, was documented with other photographs, produced by contemporary artists, turned commercial agents and salesmen of *touristic* prints *avant-la-lettre*. The inescapable J. Antonio, a Bangkok based photographer who had first worked as a drawing technician for the Royal Siamese Railway Department, also figures here. One would almost wish to be his inheritor, if only his master collection of negatives for the prints that traveled worldwide in suitcases of numerous travelers, could be located!

We should however not forget that Marthe Bassenne and *Le Tour du Monde* were solidly French — '*colon*' we might add. Such feelings of, almost too neutral admiration for these clever people who managed to remain a buffer state between Indochina and British Burma, as we can read between the lines in Bassenne's brief report on who controls trade in Bangkok, remind us of the wounded pride of the French colonial interests, so aptly frustrated by the support to Siam of some other, unmentionable arch-neutralists, the Belgians. One must never forget what lies behind, and takes precedence over, the observer's eyes. A French mind in a French body. And that is what we do not have here, a body to go with this French woman's account of impressions and feelings —'*maintes fois caressés*' too, no doubt, during that long period from 15 December 1909 until 27 January 1912, the publication date of the account. Probably read many more times than just that one time, admitted in January 1910: 'I open this *journal de route* once more to add to it a melancholic note...' One of her many friends on the road: her cook—unable to cook, because no Siamese would sell any scrap of fresh food to a despicable French woman—had died, and, even for a Westerner, dying is a bit like traveling to that other strange land, into another adventure, into a new life.

Dr. Walter E. J. Tips
October 1994

The colophon of Le Tour du Monde

Sources of Illustrations

Most of the seventy pictures, originally published in the magazine, have been reproduced here from the French edition in which the travel account was first published. However, some have been taken from an abbreviated version of the original text that had been published in 1913, in the Dutch equivalent of *Le Tour du Monde*. This magazine was called *De Aarde en Haar Volken*—The Earth and its Peoples— and it was published in the Netherlands by H. D. Tjeenk Willink & Zoon from Haarlem.

In crediting photographs to photographers, other than herself, it seems Marthe Bassenne has not always been accurate: some of the pictures incorporated in the section on Bangkok look remarkably well like J. Antonio's. Yet, his name does not figure in the caption. Such oversights apart, the photographs present some unusual aspects of traveling upcountry in those days.

The map, with the route of the travels of Marthe Bassenne and her husband indicated by a heavy broken line, was originally published in the French version. Nothing has been altered.

In Laos and Siam

by

Mme Marthe Bassenne

Le Tour du Monde, Volume XVIII, New Series, No. 4, 27 January 1912; No. 5, 3 February 1912; No. 6, 10 February 1912; No. 7, 17 February 1912; No. 8, 24 February 1912; and No. 9, 2 March 1912; pages 37-108.

In Laos and Siam

Map of Indochina with the route of Marthe Bassenne's journey.

xiv

Chapter 1

The Lower Mekong and the Rapids of Kemmarat

On the Bassac—The railway of the Island Khône—The loading of the Garcerie—*Laotian huts in Pakse—In the rapids of Kemmarat—The trips by pirogue—In Savanaket—The missionaries of the Mekong—The gold of Laos—How one builds a pirogue—Crocodile hunting*

31 October 1909

Leaving Saigon on October 27, we fulfill a desire which we have toyed with many times since our arrival in Cochinchina, i.e., a visit to Laos. Curiosity draws us to this relatively recently annexed region, of which the inhabitants have not yet lost their primitive customs upon contact with Europeans. We especially want to visit the Luang-Prabang country bordering Burma, and of which one hears so many strange things.

This journey usually takes three months. There are no roads. The sole entry point to our destination is along the Mekong. This immense waterway is amongst the largest in the world. It descends from Tibet and covers a distance of more than 4,000 kilometers. It sows rapids and is famous for its overflows too. The primary mode of transportation is the slow pirogue. Nevertheless, every year, during the short time that the medium high waters last, the *Messageries Fluviales* of Cochinchina manage to make a few journeys by steamer up to Vientiane, at 1,400 kilometers from the mouth of the stream. However, one has to resort again to pirogues to cover the 600 kilometers that separate Vientiane from Luang-Prabang, since navigation on this stretch is not organized for public service.

Luckily, Mr. Mahé, the amiable *résident superieur* of Laos, has offered my husband two places in a government rowboat that will bring him from Vientiane to Luang-Prabang at the end of November. This is the precise time when the height of the waters allows an attempt to cross the rapids. For us now, we must try to arrive in Vientiane by way of the *Messageries Fluviales*, early enough to make use of this unexpected offer. Big festivities are announced in Luang-Prabang for the end of the twelfth Laotian month, which is for 17, 18, 19 and 20 November. If the waters do not descend too early and if we do not fail on a great rapid, we will be there. The lowering of the waters will certainly prevent us from returning by the same route. However, it is our intention to leave the Mekong in Upper Laos and to travel overland to reach the Menam, by following the scarce tracks that have been worn out of the creepers of the forest by bullock caravans. The Menam, which runs from the North to the South, across Siam, will lead us to Bangkok.

We take along our cook, Ba, an old devoted Annamite, who knows a bit of Chinese with us, since Laos and Siam have been invaded by Chinese merchants. Also, we happen to hire, as boy-interpreter, a young Cambodian of Siamese origin, by the name of Kaé, who, proud of his new appointment, struts about in a costume the color of young green shoots and begins each sentence with, '*Moi bien connaisse.*'[1] His duties as an attendant, the care for the horses, the Siamese language and its derivative, Laotian—he knows it all. We will see him at work.

It is possible that we will have to battle against difficulties and face some dangers before making it to our destination. The rapids have rendered many victims; the tiger inhabited forest is full of fevers. At least the first few days of our journey have passed by in the greatest calm. Two boats of the *Messageries Fluviales* have brought us in four days up the lower course of the Mekong covering 700 kilometers. After the low and swampy shores of the delta of Cochinchina, in Cambodia we have seen banks arise which border this immense tablecloth of water of several kilometers. From this water, which is charged with alluvium during this season, emerge big islands and beacons in masonry that indicate the channel for the boats.

Today there was a complete change in scenery. We no longer saw the cultivated banks and the Cambodian huts perched on piles. There were only big trees on all sides; we navigated in dense jungle. Our boat, the *Bassac,* has in effect left Stung Treng, the capital of the last province of Cambodia, this morning to enter a real forest that the Mekong covers at high and middle waters. One calls it the drowned forest. Nothing could re-create the mysteriousness that emanates from this voyage. Big trees emerge alone, smooth and straight, like the trunks of an immense forest of pines, pressed together here, or further apart there, in mysterious lanes which vanish into some unknown enchanted clearing . . . . The leaves fall silently on the moving waterway, not one cry of a bird, no other noises but the lapping of the water against the bark. Under this archway of greenery, the boat appears to advance without goal, without direction, as if lost in a labyrinth. At 11 a.m. we seemed to escape from the shady maze, as we approached the Island of Khône.

Plate 1 *A missionary with a group of his folk, waiting for us on the bank of a village in Pak Sane.*

It is here, at the Southern border of Laos, that we leave the *Bassac*: navigation is impossible between the Island of Khône and the lands separated by impassable waterfalls—barriers that limit the lower reaches of the Mekong. These are the first obstacles met with when trying to penetrate Laos. The problem of their passage has been solved by the establishment of a small railway line which crosses through the island from the South to the North, i.e. four kilometers. At the Northern landing, we find a boat, which has been transported, piece by piece, up to this point and has been reassembled on the spot, to enable us to rejoin the Laotian Mekong.

3

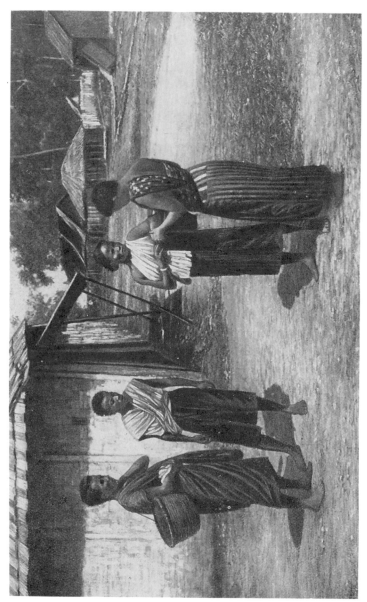

Plate 2 *Laotian women in a village of Lower Laos. The men and women of Cambodia and Laos cut their hair to a crew-cut.*

An army of coolies stacked the merchandise in small, open train-cars wherein we piled in, together with the locals, balancing ourselves on the luggage in utter chaos. The train pulled us, struggling along, grating and with the clashing sound of steel, across the island that is covered by assorted teak trees mixed with bamboo, the branches of which brush across our face. The temperature was extremely high and the sun which filtered through the trees evaporated putrid and fevered fumes from the entangled undergrowth. Sweat caked my hair under my colonial hat. Through my clothes the heat roasted my arms and the mosquitoes, profiting from my listlessness attacked me as they pleased, all over my hands and face which I surrendered to their mercy.

Then, upon landing in North Khône, the coolies loaded our new boat, the *Garcerie*. It is a boat only thirty-two meters long. A bigger boat would not be able to navigate through the abrupt bends of the channel we are following. We will be quite crammed because about a hundred locals, of which fifty are Annamites on their way to work at the removal of rocks at the Kemmarat rapids, have to be accommodated. We also have to bother with merchandise that is too heavy for the pirogues and which has been waiting for the waters to rise high enough to allow one of the rare journeys of the *Garcerie*. Bags of cement and enormous crates are taken from the launch and placed on the bridge of the ship. On starboard I bump into the firewood for the ship's engine; on backboard I stumble over the pieces of a dredge that will be used to extract gold dust from a tributary of the Mekong.

The locals climbed on the roof of the ship's cabin, and squatted there amidst their packages, their sleeping mats, their small suitcases, their every possession. Among them there is a Laotian woman from Luang-Prabang who returns to her country with a baby of four years. Our co-passengers know her. She had, not so long ago, the reputation of a great beauty, but, the climate ages women before they are twenty years old. She confirmed that the child is her adopted son, bought for eight *piasters* from needy parents. The small child has more refined traits, more suppleness than the young Laotians and his bronzed face is brightened up by two big impish, hardly slanted, black eyes. I asked him to embrace me in his own language. He tended his little face and planted a big kiss on my cheek. I concluded from this that he was a French half-breed. The children of the locals do not know this affectionate gesture of the kiss.

5

Talking about European passengers, the *Garcerie* never had so many. First, there are two officers of the militia and lieutenant Marc of the Geographical Service of Indochina; all three are going to Savanaket. Then Mr. Lester, a navy lieutenant, who was placed at the disposal of Public Works (Bridges and Roads of Indochina) and who works as a section chief in the service of navigation on the Kemmarat rapids—which do not hold any secrets for him whatsoever. He has crossed them during all seasons, risking one hundred times to be thrown against the rocks or to be drowned by the whirlpools. Finally, we have aboard for just one hour, lieutenant Berger of the infantry who is also employed by Public Works. He is building a twenty kilometer road on the left bank of the river. It starts down stream from the Island of Khône and ends up stream near the village of Huai Kinak. This road is destined to replace the small railway line of the Island of Khône when it will be furnished with a Renard train.[2] In this way one will avoid the problems of navigation which, during part of the year, are serious on the Northern side of the island. The river-bed of the Mekong stretches here over a width of ten kilometers, seven kilometers of which are islands.

For a moment, at Ban Huai Kinak, we enjoy the hospitality of the lieutenant in a house ingeniously decorated by his lovely wife. A local, seated under the verandah, serenaded us by playing the *khêne*, the national musical instrument of Laos. It is an assembly of seven, nine or thirteen bamboo sticks of various lengths. The musician blows into a mouth-piece and moves his fingers over holes made in the bamboo tubes, improvising in an infinitely melancholic and inadequate way, a slow, monotonous chant that sounds like the uncertain and searching manifestation of his far away soul. With the complicity of a stormy atmosphere, a weariness was invading us; every one wished to have a siesta that would dispel the sensations induced by this vague and soft chant. However, the ship-bell summoned us. We had to rejoin the *Garcerie* that will sail until 2 a.m. on this route without pitfalls.

There was a short stop at the Island of Kong, the station of a resident, or rather a *commissariat* because, in Laos, the provincial administrators are called commissioners of the French Government. Then, it was twilight, the short twilight of the tropics that quickly makes room for the night. I rested my elbows on the front of the small boat, and I could hardly distinguish anything of the stream beyond the circle of light projected by the lamp of the pilot. And now, here in the mute shade, a subtle and delicate perfume reached me from the earth: it was as if the river was sown with tubers and carnations in a somewhat faded grassland. It goes to the head, it intoxicates the senses and I was nearly taken in by it. Then, the perfume evaporated like if it was swept away by a jealous breeze never to return. Yet, it permeated the air once again even more penetrating, more mysterious. However, no flower beds decorated the bank, no hand has mowed a missing grassland, only the inviolate forest extends infinitely on the river bank and this scent that surprised me, is simply the scent of Laos. It seems that it will follow me all along the stream and that I will also inhale it much later when I will sleep at night in the forest. Is it produced by the odoriferous woods of Laos or by its jungle vines, or by so many orchids— precious parasites of these trees—of which some specimens are sold for the price of gold in England? But, wherever it comes from, I respond to this salute of the Laotian earth and I receive it like a friendly omen for a good journey.

1 November 1909

When we woke we saw before us Bassac on the right bank of the Mekong. Formerly, the capital of a Laotian Kingdom, it is today the most important village of Lower Laos. It has been built at the foot of a chain of small, forested mountains upon which a bluish haze gently sits this morning. Siam has only ceded Bassac, with a strip of territory on the right bank, to us in 1904, and the capital of the French province is upstream, at Pakse where we will arrive in eleven hours' time.

The vast, deserted stream, widened still by the mouth of the Sedone, is calm here like a lake and the immense forest, like a coat over the mountains of the opposite bank in the distance, exudes an oppressive gloom. Gradually, the sadness of the landscape grew bigger still: a storm was approaching from beyond the horizon, suddenly striated by rain, and the thunder broke, arousing sinister echoes. This evening of 1 November, which in France we dedicate to the dead, seemed to me to be singularly lugubrious and as if haunted by the shadows of the unlucky who sleep their fitful sleep at the depths of this murderous stream, in the rapids of Kemmarat that we were then approaching.

Pakse, 2 November 1909

By clearing a corner of the forest, some houses for the civil servants of the *commissariat* have recently been built for the local guard and for an ambulance

Plate 3 *At the entrance of the submerged forest, there is one of the beacons in brick-work that mark the channel for the boats (Photo Simon).*

that will offer refuge to Europeans of Lower Laos who fall ill. These stone houses have already suffered this year from invading waters. Despite the elevation of the banks they were immersed in 2.50 meters of water during the floods.

However, much more than the French style houses, my interest was drawn to the Laotian village with its gracious huts that the locals build or repair under my very eyes. As soon as the materials are assembled, they drive tree trunks into the earth and on these poles, at about two meters above the soil, they establish a floor made of bamboo trellis which vibrates under the weight of the body and thus gives the impression of a suspended hammock. White mats form the partitions and the roof is thatched with rice straw. Then, the owner climbs to his home by the small chicken ladder that serves as a staircase, installs his rice basket and sleeping mat. From then onwards he lives in the sweetest *far-niente*, without ambitious desires, almost without needs, cultivating but rice and fishing only the fish necessary for his food, while earning only a bit of money to enable him to buy opium.

Indeed, the arrival of a boat and her subsequent loading, are for the locals easy ways of gaining a few small coins. However, their laziness at work is amusing. Where two porters are necessary, six step forward. Only the two most naive ones support the load, the others simulate an effort, make gestures and, especially, shout like possessed men. Moreover, these are men without muscles under the fine blue or red tattoos, that decorate their bodies. All Laotians are tattooed down to their knees. It's their costume without which a young man would not be able to please a woman. Since this tattooing is very painful, opium serves as an anesthetic and the patient smokes, without relenting, during the fifteen days of the operation.

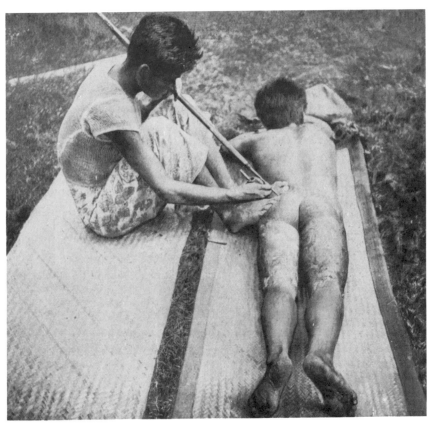

Plate 4 *All the Laotians have themselves tattooed (Photo Ragnez).*

Among all these peoples of Indochina, I experience the same apprehension to distinguish men from women, because their identical haircuts mislead me. The Annamites wear their hair long and turned back in buns on the crown. However, men and women of Cambodia and Laos have crew cuts. This fashion was earlier imposed by the Siamese, conquerors of these countries, who had the heads of women shaved off while they themselves had short hair. Nevertheless, young Laotian girls now retain their long, black hairdo and tie it on the crowns of their heads, very high, as a smooth shell that rests partially on one ear. It makes their small, pale faces more saucy. A crew cut indicates that the woman is married. Instead of the black silk costumes that the Annamites and their women wear, here we have a medley of light silks rolled around brown bodies, which the men pull up between the legs to fashion into a small *sampot,* or shortpants—also used by the Siamese and the Cambodians. The women, in general, prefer to let their fabrics drop to their loins and they half cover their breasts . . .

Having left Pakse at noon, before long we reached the confluence of the Se Moun, the only large tributary of the river to the right. Starting from this point, over 850 kilometers, this right bank which was French from Bassac onwards, becomes Siamese and the Mekong forms the border between Siamese Laos and French Laos. We made a stopover for the night at Ban Koun where we increased our load of firewood in preparation for the rapids that we will cross tomorrow. Some miserable huts constitute the whole village. The inhabitants squat around what one could call the public square: a beat-up space in the middle of which the buffaloes are posted together to be better able to guard them against attempts at theft during the night. For the first time, I see buffaloes with pink hairs that bare a striking contrast, by their faded robes, to their brothers in black fur.

3 November 1909

There is much commotion, starting from 3 a.m. in preparation for the dangerous crossing of the Kemmarat rapids. The stokers ignite the firebox, the mechanic checks the boiler and, since loading the high part of the boat would be dangerous during the passage of the rapids, the commissioner orders the locals, on the roof, to come down and he distributes them over the lower bridge. They are prohibited from moving, in anticipation of a panic situation that may hurl them all over the same side.

We left at daybreak. At 7 a.m. a scream was heard: 'The rapid!' I ran to the front. There, in front of us, were the bars of foam, the rocky points, the whirlpools that—presenting themselves in a straight line—block the stream perpendicularly. It will be necessary not to submit to the raging current and to navigate across the reefs in such a way that the boat does not hit any submerged rock, nor let itself be

Plate 5 *An indigenous man presents us with a serenade on his* khêne, *the national instrument of Laos.*

11

engulfed by any whirlpools or swollen holes that attract all that drifts, crippled by the water. The waves rose upwards ahead of us, offensive. The water entered at the front, the lower bridge was swept away. The stream swelled under the boat like a breathing flank. To the right and the left, depressions were hollowed out, forming large bowls in which dim crests of foam appeared to boil. Not once did the captain leave the rudder. An old Laotian pilot, wearing red, signaled, from time to time, a short word of caution extending a skinny sibyl arm to show the way. The boat veered, inclining sharply as it lunged forward in successive spurts as it struggled in new whirlpools. We advanced forward, but barely. The steam engine spewed its breath. All the powers of the boat—her brain power and physical stamina—were stretched to the limit in the fierce battle . . . Finally, in a last compelling effort, it righted itself and all was at rest—the din of the rapids and the incessant hum of the boiler. The blanket of water that surrounded us was calm. The line of foam, once again violated, closed in behind us.

The old pilot, squatted on the bridge, waiting for the next rapid, revealing from his cover a horribly deformed face: forehead and nose flattened, jaws jutting out like a chimpanzee. The fall of a bunch of coconuts had him disfigured thus. It is not an infrequent mishap in Laos. The good La Fontaine had not foreseen it when he wrote his fable *Le Gland et La Citrouille*.[3]

I complained a bit for having my feet made wet by the gushing water that inundated the bridge and everyone shouted out: 'You are short of training!' What is a foot-bath compared to the miseries one endures when one has to ascend the Kemmarat rapids by pirogue? We will start by day-break, together with the merchandise on the bottom of the small vessel. Some twenty escorts are to pull the pirogue by a rope when it is in the low waters and sometimes the escorts even carry the pirogue with all her contents in their arms. In the high waters, these unlucky escorts are no longer able to even tow her. They then advance with the aid of sticks, armed with harpoons which they hook onto the soil and on submerged trees. Sometimes they lose several hours of work because the point of support of the harpoons has given way and they have been taken adrift. So much effort is involved in advancing three kilometers a day! In the morning, one can see the sand bank or the rock that will be reached in the evening.

A descend by pirogue is not advisable. Speed is not lacking, on the contrary. Especially in very high waters when the flood line reaches twenty-nine meters in

Plate 6 *The falls of Pap'Haeng, Island of Khône (Photo Berger).*

Plate 7 *Falls of the Mekong, at low water, in the Bay of Saint-Marguerite, Island of Khône (Photo Berger).*

13

certain points. In all the rapids the pirogue moves like an arrow. It's an ardent battle between the skill of the rowers and the pitfalls of the stream which seeks victims. Then, one is not very concerned about the tons of water entering the boat. Of prime concern is not to crash into a rock, fall into a whirlpool, or, get sucked into the hollows of a funnel . . . . The logs of teak wood, thrown into the stream, reappear without much damage 300 meters downstream. But a similar immersion kills a man. And if, with much effort, one escapes this center of attraction, it is only after having been spun around in circles for hours. This was the case with an officer who accompanied, in this macabre dance, the corpse of a drowned person. How many have never come to the surface again! Each rapid is like a common grave of unlucky victims because one seldom finds the corpse. Regarding the merchandise that is enveloped up by the stream, one no longer counts on it. One day, while trying to recover some shipwrecked Decauville equipment,[4] the Laotians salvaged a case of champagne and another with pots of jam that had, beyond doubt, been lying on a bed of mud with no trace of the Decauville equipment!

'But do not believe,' somebody adds charitably, 'that on the *Garcerie* we are not in any danger. There is the danger of being stranded on a sand bank where the boat, transformed before us into the raft of the Medusa, will be entrenched until the high waters of the following summer. There is the danger of seeing it ripped apart, torn by the rocks at the bottom, and, if the pressure is not strong enough, there is a danger of being swirled about, overturned with the tail in the air, tossed about like a simple pirogue in the abysses of the stream.'

While I forgot the present engrossed in these tales, the old Laotian had silently regained his place, close to the captain. Suddenly, I was abruptly flung to the ground and rolled to the other side. I cried out . . . this time, the locals did the same . . . .'Shut up,' the captain abruptly said, 'it's nothing: just the small caress of a rock!' We were in a rapid! Hopefully the leak won't be serious! This question, however, did not seem to be the captain's most important preoccupation and he remained carefully at the helm. The rock was clearly visible, on the left side, just next to the boat, and to the right we were by the edge of an immense whirlpool. We dared not advance, the situation was critical, the minutes long . . . .

Finally, Mr. Lester rushed to a crank, the boat backed up a bit, while turning, then it advanced softly while bracing the edge of the whirlpool. And now, well

Plate 8 *A pirogue with passengers in low waters. In the morning, one points out the sand bank that one reaches only in the evening (Photo Berger).*

disengaged, it definitely passed the Keng Song Khône. At this moment, a passenger who had just visited the hold, signaled a leak but there was little danger. We had taken in some tons of water only. I let Lester's actions, which I did not understand, be explained to me. He had stopped the functioning of one of the two screws when the boat, stopped by the power of the current, no longer obeyed the rudder. Disconnecting one screw for a few seconds had made possible the turning necessary for the relaunch in the right direction.

At the third rapid, due to an error of the local stokers, the pressure suddenly weakened. The boat did not advance and seemed to hesitate, I noted this by observing reference markers on the banks. Will it drift away with the current? .... Go to it stokers! .... The pressure increased again, the passage was made .... It surprised me that we were still gracing the whirlpools. Was it to stir the passengers' emotions? Not at all. It seems inevitable. The boat can pass in the openings of the bar and downstream from an opening there is always a whirlpool.

The series of rapids that followed were less dangerous. At 11 a.m., leaving behind us the Keng Yapeu, the last large rapid we were to encounter, we penetrated what one calls 'the corridors of the Mekong'. Here the stream narrows until it is only 300 meters wide. Its depth is frightening. A wall of rock, eighty to hundred meters high, cut by caves and from which waterfalls emerge, rises vertically from all sides. Enormous flat stones overhang them as if haphazardly laid there by a giant. How would one compare this funnel to the gorges of the torrents?[5] Some of the gorges appear to be even more ferocious because of their tightened faces which only sparingly dispense air and light. Nothing could, however, compare with the grandiose image portrayed by this natural canal, its formidable mass of water gushing down between titanic walls.

At the exit of this pass, two beautiful rapids renewed my emotions of the morning, with their rocks, strewn in the middle of the stream, around which the water cascaded. Finally, at 6 p.m. we stopped for the night at Ban Tapane. On the riverband, there was the melancholy silhouette of a European—an employee of the local Postal Services who was repairing the telegraphic lines.

Since leaving the corridors the stream has widened a little. On the embankments of the river, even the smallest piece of land is cultivated and cotton is grown by the locals of the forest villages. This is because the embankments of the Mekong, sometimes twenty to thirty meters high, are remarkably fertile due to the flood time alluvium deposits. Also, the Laotians have a practice similar to the riverside residents of the Nile. When the water recedes, the few inhabitants of the neighborhood arrive, sow and take advantage of this natural fertilizer for their plantations. As a result cotton and other vegetables color the banks green until the next invasion of the waters. This did not imply that the bank was deserted that evening—small monkeys wandered about in full safety!

How different this is from the severe loneliness of the landscapes of the Delta in Cochinchina! The climate itself is completely different. The temperature here drops to +10 degrees Centigrade for two or three months of the year and falls much lower, it seems, in northern Laos. The air was heavy, saturated with humidity, and a light breeze, unknown in Saigon, whipped our faces. It was delightful. And the scent, the sweet scent of Laos reappeared tonight from the stream, like compensation for our day of efforts. At the same time, a sensation of mystery, of intense, keenly felt, melancholy descended upon us. Our boat seemed to be the only false note in this wild decorum. Nevertheless, she deserved to be in Laos to which she brought, despite so many obstacles, the impatiently awaited elements of well-being stored in her hull. All night long I heard the aspiration of the pump that exhausted the hold of water.

4 November 1909

One or two very dangerous rapids in low waters, but insignificant during this season, close the series of rapids of Kemmarat, unjustly named after a Siamese village of the right bank which, in reality, is situated upstream from these rapids. After having left Mr. Lester and his burdensome fifty Annamites behind in the hamlet of Ban Aprat Sun, we arrived in Savanaket at 4 p.m. It is a charming little post, created by the French, with welcomming colonial houses and flowering gardens, bordering the Mekong, along an alley of wild coconut trees.

Mr. D.-S., resident clerk, received us on behalf of the commissioner of the Government and placed his house at our disposal without allowing us to make use of the *sala*, or guest house, a straw hut, which in Laos replaces the hotels wherein travelers install their bivouac beds, and unpack their provisions. A change in the timetable of the *Messageries Fluviales* obliged us to reside here for three days, sharing, not without remorse, the provisions which the French of Savanaket obtain so tediously.

Savanaket, 5 November 1909

This was the starting point of a route that will connect, when it will be completed, the Mekong with the Sea of Annam across the Annamite mountains, while the precise route of the railway line is being studied. The construction of this railway line of 350 kilometers is the dream of the Laotians. In this way, the difficult problem of the navigation of the Kemmarat rapids will be solved.

We gratefully enjoyed the attention we were paid. They made us forget the emotions of the rapids. But our boys appreciated the calmness of Savanaket perhaps even more than us. Kaé, our Siamese boy, adopted an air of importance: he had found friends. He knew the *Chao Muong* (the local governor) and he no longer needed to make this known. And Ba, our cook, disoriented and very far from his Cochinchina, unable to understand Laotian, passed his days sitting in the shade, in the garden of our host. 'Very naughty Mekong,' he said. One cannot extract more than that from him.

7 November 1909

Yesterday, we witnessed the departure of the *Garcerie* which is returning down river to Khône. The leaks in his hull have been packed with cement as well as possible. How many more times will this brave small vessel renew its bravery before it wins its retirement, twisted and dented. Or perhaps it will have a heroic end at the bottom of the Kemmarat rapids. It has disappeared in the distance in the early morning light, passing the floats of teak wood or bamboo which, descending from the high regions, glide in the middle of the stream, projecting a half-dead cock tied in the front as a propitiation sacrifice of the locals to the evil goddesses of the water. And today we will ourselves embark on the *Colombert* , a brother of the *Garcerie*, which provides the service of the superior reach of the Mekong, between Savanaket and Vientiane, 500 kilometers that one can safely sail all year round by steamer.

The widened stream flows in the middle of a sparsely inhabited valley covered with forests and the jungle. Our only distraction on a long day of monotonous navigation, was the view in the distance of a chain of rocky and denuded mountains, a strange chaos of collapsed pyramids, of cones, peaks, and arrows which called to mind the rocks of the bay of Along, that marvel of the Indochinese coast.

Then comes the night and with her a large flock of flying bugs crashed into the boat while it docked at the French post of Pak Hin Boun. Our feet crushed them on the bridge and, since we could not keep them out of our food, we renounced dinner. After we had sent ashore the mail of Pak Hin Boun, the captain decided to advance all night to compensate for a long stop-over tomorrow during which we would be obliged to unload the merchandise at Pak Sane.

8 November 1909

We arrived at the small Laotian village of Pak Sane at 3 p.m. On the bank, a missionary awaited us with a group of his flock. Is it under his pressure, and the dictates of Western prudishness, that the Laotian women converts have sacrificed their transparant shawl which traditionally covered their young breasts? Esthetics

Plate 9 *Embarking on the pirogues (Photo Péri).*

loses everything by it, because the shawl is replaced by some sort of cotton vest which, in France, we commonly call a *caraco*.[6]

Seventy missionaries are, in this manner, distributed on the two banks of the Mekong, under the jurisdiction of a bishop who lives on the Siamese side. There is a missionary among each small local built-up area. A hundred meters away from us, on a knoll that dominates the village, is a retreat: an enclosure in the midst of which an odd chapel in wood is erected. But the Laotians' total indifference to religious matters results in infrequent conversions. Especially, they are little sincere. It should be well-understood that, in Laos, just like in Algeria and Madagascar, the Anglican priests compete with the Catholic priests and they too seek to attract the locals. Without fear of penetrating the interior of the country with their women and children, they can, due to studies in medicine, tend to the body and soul. The French missionaries do a little bit of everything. For example, they supply firewood to our boats. Several times we have accosted their little estates for wood that has been prepared on the river bank. We in turn hand over the mail to these lonely hearts. As a representative of the Gold-digging Company which is being formed, the missionary of Pak Sane receives today the dredge which has been bothering us since Khône.

Until today, all attempts at setting up a lucrative business in gold exploitation in Laos have been in vain. Nevertheless, according to the prospectors, there is gold everywhere in the country. However, it is so widely spread that one does not find veins that are sufficiently productive. Moreover, there is a total dearth of labour for the strenuous extraction because of the laziness of the locals. Thus, there remains the gold that the rivers sweep down. The dredge that we are bringing, could only just compete with the primitive methods that the Laotian gold-washers adopt. They effectively separate the gold from the mud and the sand and they entrust it then to their goldsmiths who transforms it into heavy jewelry for their women. Do not offer a Laotian woman any imitation of the precious metal; she would scorn it, preferring fragile hangers of scented flowers if she were too poor to cover herself with real gold. The Laotians also gild their Buddhas. If the faithful can not completely cover the God that they invoke, at least they will offer him as homage, very small pieces of gold glued about everywhere, in yellow patches on his nose, his forehead, his navel. We have seen in almost every hamlet where we stopped, Buddhas decorated in this way.

On a whim, I used the last hours of the day to ascend the banks of the Nam Sane, a beautiful river which plunges at this point into the Mekong. The waters here display a perfect brightness and clearness that form an absolute contrast to the waters of the large stream, always cloudy and muddy. On the trees on the bank are moored a few of these slender pirogues. The Laotians are skilled artisans who construct these boats out of tree trunks twelve to fifteen meters in length. On a level plane, using an ax or saw, they cut a large longitudinal cavity, stopping at one meter from each end. Then with the help of wooden struts they separate bit-by-bit the two borders of the cavity in which they make a fire to render the wood more supple. The largest widening is carved in the middle of the piece where one obtains an empty space considerably larger than the diameter of the tree, while the two other extremities run together into a spindle. The whole vessel is subject to a thorough finishing touch. The inner surfaces become very thin and of uniform width. These boats boast an elegance that small boats of other countries do not possess. And, if the pirogue must transport passengers, they cover it up, in its median section, with mats placed on half-hoops, for shelter from the rain and the sun.

Plate 10 *Lao types from the borders of the Mekong (Photo Péri).*

The pirogue-rowers had guessed my desire and vied for the privilege to conduct us. For an hour, we sailed up stream the Nam Sane which seemed to join cascading waterfalls and rapids. Here, however, it flows in shadowy creeks, sometimes becoming a clear mirror for the forest. Our passage caused commotion along the banks, flushed with vegetation, animated with the life of the beasts which inhabit them, and which were at the most hundred meters away. While the high, hollow bamboos, crushed together in the breeze, sing like wind harps, auburn monkeys jump from branch to branch and the undergrowth undulates from the flight of wild hen. The river itself was so populated with fish that they, being deranged by our oars, jumped on the banks where we collected them by hand.

Plate 11 *Return from fishing.*

9 November 1909

The departure was at 3 a.m. At sunset, on the sandy river-banks, crocodiles stretched their long, scaly bodies, the color of dried mud. One of the attractions of traveling up the Mekong was to shoot at these large saurians. They testified a profound indifference to our gun-shots when the bullets did not reach them.[7] They did not even lift their heads at the whistling of the projectile. But, when hit, they instantly dived with supreme skill. At the surface of the water then appeared a large pool of blood and they died at the bottom of the stream where their corpses served as food for their brothers.

The valley has widened even more and the mountains on the horizon have disappeared. Around us were the planes, or, rather the forest glades—the insipid jungle. Along the deserted banks flocks of marabous trailed their wings as they marched with small measured steps, like old invalids. Or, they stood around on one leg, in a straight line, just like soldiers in a parade, as we passed them. Suddenly, obeying I know not what signal, a fraction of them separated, took wing simultaneously, and aligned themselves further ahead in an advance post. Then, the entire flock took flight and its compact group stained the horizon. For some hours there was no other trace of life around us. Then, by evening, the banks were full of people—construction wharves for pirogues employed many locals. Vientiane was no longer far away.

The first part of our sojourn has ended: we rejoined Mr. Mahé at the appointed date for our departure to Luang-Prabang.

Plate 12 *On the Mekong, close to Luang-Prabang, locals on their way by pirogue to the festivities of the twelfth month.*

Chapter 2

From Vientiane to Luang-Prabang
The Ruins of Vientiane

The residence of Vientiane—Walks in the city—On the La
Grandière—*In the rapids—Arrival at Luang-Prabang—Paklay—
Regarding tigers*

10 November 1909

Vientiane! The *Colombert* sailed in at 8.30 a.m. and we climbed the banks not
without trouble, because the embankment was so much the higher since the level
of the water had fallen. Ah! This receding of the water, how it worried us! Our first
question to Mr. Mahé who waited for us on the bank, testified our worries: 'Can
one go to Luang-Prabang?'—'Yes, yes, the *La Grandière* is ready, you will leave
tomorrow.'

We walked towards the residence: three charming pavilions in the middle of a
flowering grassland, constructed where earlier the palace of the old kings of
Vientiane stood. We took asylum in a wing that is reserved for guests. The central
pavilion was inhabited by the *résident superieur*. It drew special attention to its
very large hall that runs all along the front of the building—a sort of waiting room
or atrium—where earlier the local chiefs assembled and, along the perimeter of
which, are aligned enormous, bronze Buddhas. These statues stand on platforms
in the three classical postures: reclining Buddhas, Buddhas standing in the preaching
position, and Buddhas seated cross-legged, one arm pulled back to the navel, the
other extended to the toe. They all had the same arched waist, the same graceful
body; the head, with fine traits, with a fixed smile was crowned by a pointed tiara
or a skullcap formed out of some sort of rounded balls arranged in regular rows.

They are able to rest in their own country, these dethroned gods, but, how many others, torn away from the ruins, have left for unforeseen destinations! Previously, no European would leave Laos without taking in his baggage some specimen of a lost art and the pagodas were thus being denuded. The time is not far when the Laotian gods will be everywhere, except in Laos. The Administration has strictly forbidden this exodus. The Customs of Khône refuse the passage of every Buddha, big or small, that gets there. It concerns us very little since we have never thought of encumbering ourselves with such voluminous travel souvenirs. We are content to admire the Buddhas at home, in the midst of all these old ruins that tell of a prosperous past.

Poor country! At the onset of our excursion today in the old Vientiane, we understood the desolation that was doomed its fate. Before, it was the capital of a flourishing Laotian kingdom, as Luang-Prabang was too. What is left of this today? The bellicose Siamese came during the last century, destroyed the temples, seized their riches and harnessed in chains women and children whom these gentle people had not been able to defend. The conquered were dispatched to Bangkok as slaves—yet unbeknown to them—and the devastated country was left to mourn in solitude. Here, just like in Angkor, the tropical vegetation has thrown a veil over so many disasters. Unfortunately, the roots of the giant trees have continued the Siamese work of destruction, deceitfully weakening the foundations of the temples that were still standing, and the intertwining lianas have beheaded the precarious frontons! No trace of the ancient civilization would have remained visible had Eastern Laos not become French in 1893. As soon as the country had been organized, our residents mused upon fighting with the jungle for these remainders of the old capital, to lift it out of its ruins, to re-populate the city. Moreover, the creation of this new Vientiane, has resulted in its becoming the administrative capital of the whole of Laos. Thus, little-by-little the city has regained its importance, but, what conscientious efforts, what determination and energy is still necessary to render it its past splendour! They hacked across this jungle that was a city, to pave roads along which, alternating with the bamboo huts, are erected stone houses in which public services are housed. This is a slow process done within the limits of the budgetary resources that one has to defend every inch of the way, each year. Laos is so far away! The last newcomer in our Indochinese Empire is forgotten—deliberately, it is said—to the benefit of the other territories. Luckily, Mr. Mahé has confidence: confidence in the future of the country, confidence in the possibility to improve navigation on the Mekong,

Plate 13 *A street in Vientiane.*

and towards the realization of these hopes he gives the best of himself, fighting at the same time against the apprehensions of many and the apathy of the locals.

Our walk lasted into the night. Haphazardly we met with smashed open walls, demolished enclosures, and sculptures that were buried under brambles, which we stumbled over. All these old temples—*wats* in Laotian language—were constructed of small, fired, earthen bricks, imperfectly baked and coated with a mortar so hard, so resistant, that the workers have carved it as if they carve stone. Everywhere fine scrolls decorate the cornices and the bases. Menacing snakes and horned dragons spiral around the columns, all made with this marvelous mortar. We must note that it was reinforced, since they found iron bars in the bodies of these fantastic beasts. In some places, underlining the sculptures, pieces of ceramic—usually reflecting blues or whites that the fine dust of centuries has dulled or which crumbled in days of disaster—are encrusted in the cement.

Certainly, the same inspiration that created the monuments of Angkor, the pearl of Cambodia, has given birth to, some centuries ago, these ruined temples of Laos. Only Angkor, having been constructed in hard stone, has better resisted the

27

devastating onslaught of the forest, while these *wats* of Vientiane, which, one believes to be of a later date, have been demolished almost to their foundations. For example, what remains of the Phyawat? Some shaky walls, grand masks that are mutilated and turn moldy in the grass and a delightful entrance to the temple: two slender colonnades that support a pinnacle with five decayed foundation stones, ending in a pointed spire. But what refinement in the detail of the sculptures! Each part is so undercut, subdivided, and worked open in ornaments with the chisel that the whole gives the impression of the work of a goldsmith. Set in equilibrium on these two colonnades is a sort of tiara, colossal, yes, but nevertheless fragile and light because of the serration. And here, behind this pinnacle that serves as an eternal crown, appears, seated unshakably on his plinth, a giant Buddha of six to eight meters tall, surviving impassively the decaying of the temple. He is there, under the sole archway of the sky, braving the bad weathers which have smeared to his body a green leprosy. A vigorous tree, born in the debris of a wall, extends the shadow of its leaves over his head as supreme protection. It is impressive beyond belief, this image of divinity that victoriously rises up above the rubble.

Even more impressive were the three Buddhas, abandoned at the edge of the forest, along a road full of rut that loses itself in the forest. The shrubs encircle this colossus in bronze unable, however, to smother it: the three heads rise above the foliage, spreading open their branches, as if these metal statues were marching to some sanctuary. What are they doing there, on the naked soil, these old gods, when around them there is not even some debris of an enclosure left which could explain their presence? Where can one find the secret of this past, every day more obscure, more impenetrable? Mysterious statues sculpted in imperishable material does your survival matter, if humanity merciful for the human suffering of the past—can not read on your closed lips the events that have dispersed your adorers and covered your altars with blood? The calmness of your immortality makes our ignorance even more disconcerting.

The Siamese have not but dragged with them slaves; they have not but looted jewelry. There was in the Phra Keo, the most renowned of the pagodas in the Laotian country, a Buddha with an emerald head that was the glory and the protection of Vientiane. Graceful legends idolized it and we were told that the Siamese were faced with all the trouble in the world for taking it away. It grounded the boats that carried it, and disappeared to the bottom of the rivers of

Siam, then it was found back in its dear Phra Keo, mysteriously transported without anyone knowing how. Nevertheless, today it is in Bangkok and the Siamese, to reconcile it with its exile, have constructed for it, based on the plans which were discovered in the *wat* in Vientiane, a new Phra Keo that is one of the most beautiful pagodas of Bangkok. However, it is said that if a pilgrim from Vientiane comes to visit it in its new temple, the emerald Buddha will cry before his eyes, so nostalgic is it for Laos.

Of Phra Keo, there is only a ruined enclosure left, walls veiled with lianas and two porticos with delicate spires. One of these porticos has conserved intact its door in precious, carved wood, where grimacing dwarfs support costumed spirits, displaying hieratic gestures, on their heads.

A single pagoda of Vientiane remains. It is Sisaket, or the Pagoda of the Oath; the priests of a monastery are in charge of it. The chiefs of the neighboring provinces come to it, on fixed dates, to pay tribute to the representative of France, in the same gesture of vassalage that Bangkok demanded from them before. The walls of Wat Sisaket are covered with frescos that are glaringly illuminated in the style of the Far East; warriors and princes are seated astride horses—without observing the laws of perspective—and according to legends, the significance of which we find not the time to search for.

That left us to visit a strange and gigantic religious, rather well conserved, monument some kilometers away from Vientiane—the That Luong. A *that* is a very slender construction in masonry, usually in the form of a sort of a pointed church tower. It seems that the erection of these *thats* derives from an ancient cult, much earlier than Buddhism, which has merged with it and numerous traces of which are found in Laos and Siam. In as much as the Laotians do not venerate the dead as the neighboring peoples, some tombs are surmounted by *thats*. Do the ashes of a great person rest below the pile of cemented bricks that one calls the That Luong of Vientiane? Or else, was it never more than the symbol of a cult lost today or corrupted by traditions? When one emerges in the open space that isolates it from the forest, majestic, under the pale sky, it seemed to be a challenge thrown at death, at nothingness.

The That Luong consists, in reality, of several *thats*: first an enormously big, central one; then all around, on the sides of a square, thirty-two *thats* that are

Plate 14 *Vientiane. Ruins of the Pagoda of Phra Keo. The roots of the trees shatter the basis; the intertwining creepers behead the pediments (Photo Péri).*

smaller, more detailed, and that barely reach the first plinth of the giant *that*. Several of these have deteriorated somewhat, others are decapitated and there are attempts at present at striving to restore all. Finally, a dilapidated wall in ruins, atop an adjoining railing in masonry, encircles the monument. This wall, separated from the line of the *thats* by a circular path, measures, it seems to me, about seventy or eighty meters to the side. In the center of each side, a small pavilion that serves as an entrance, forms an exterior projection and offers, under its curved back roof remnants—in the fashion of the Far East—the remainders of a fine work of sculpture. All along the length of the wall inside, is a covered gallery—a sort of inner courtyard that formerly sheltered a large number of Buddhas. Twelve very beautiful images remain.

Today, one sees a resurgence of the That Luong from its torpor. Preparations for the festivities of the twelfth month, or of the Laotian New Year, are on going. We will observe them, but more impressive, in Luang-Prabang. Workers provisionally reconstruct parts of the gallery that have crumbled with bamboo and mats. They construct platforms on which actors, dancers and singers invited to the festivities, will perform as in some kind of religious fancy-fair, to which the whole of Vientiane will attend next week.

We return, crossing a race track, since recently sporting events, on which one counts for encouraging the breeding of the small Laotian horses, have been created. By denuding part of this useless jungle, it has been easy to create a marvelous race track.

That evening there was a dinner at the residence, in our honour. It reunited the civil servants of Vientiane. Among the guests were two ladies—two Frenchmen have taken their wives and children, who lightheartedly support their exile, to Laos. We were twenty-five to thirty persons gathered around the flowery table, i.e., about one-fifth of the Europeans that live in this immense Laos that is bigger than all of France. The men were wearing mildewed smokings, the women fresh diner outfits and I found this effort quite meritorious in a country so far away.

Some of our fellow citizens will be like us, passengers on the *La Grandière*. They are officers, a medical doctor and civil servants. The evening continued late in animated talk. Everyone thoroughly enjoyed the congenial atmosphere and hospitality of the attentive hostess of the house. We forgot that this state of well-being

Plate 15 *One of the portico's of the Phra Keo conserved intact with its door in sculptured wood.*

was made possible only by winning the battle against the dangerous waterway and that it may have cost the lives of some oarsmen.

Plate 16 *A half-caste baby.*

11 November 1909

At 2 p.m. when the *La Grandière*, ready to lift the anchor, summoned us, it was a brightly decorated decor on the bank that we took leave of our nice hosts. Farther away, a group of young local women chatted among themselves; they observed us; threw furtive glances at the boat, timid gestures of farewell. They were dressed in festive attire. One woman, unlike her friends, replaced the silk shawl that traditionally covered the breasts by a bolero in black velvet, embroidered with gold thread—a much appreciated dream dress. Another proudly carried a very small half-caste baby whose pretty saffron colored face was oddly framed—unexpectedly, just as in the case of French babies—by a christening cap crimped with lace and blue ribbons.

Plate 17 *The interior of a Laotian pagoda with fresco's on the walls and procession umbrella's on both sides of the altar.*

Let's hit the road. Let's leave! But not yet! At the moment of departure, we did not see Kaé. Where could we find our strange interpreter who until now, having translated nothing yet, specialized in being unpunctual? We searched the lodgings of Vientiane and after a quarter of an hour, he was brought to us, held by the ear. He had fallen asleep under the hall of the marketplace, completely drunken, so to say, on opium and rice whisky. Dazed, he collapsed on a pile of rigging ropes and the boat disappeared, full steam ahead, to make up lost time.

What convenient accomodation had been reserved for us! They have converted the *La Grandière*, which was formerly a small gun-boat, into an agreeable yacht in the service of the Administration of Laos. The engine is in the middle. The front part forms a rather large cabin that can be divided in two, as desired, by a curtain fixed to a rail. We sleep on a large divan which is on one side of the room, the other will serve as the dining room for everyone. The bathroom cabinet is in the extreme front of the boat, equipped with two comfortable wash-basins in the open air offering an opportunity for only the monkeys on the banks to spy on us. The back also forms a cabin in which four of our companions will sleep. For the two other passengers, the space on the superior deck is what remains—a small deck above our cabin, close to the rudder. Using a miller's ladder, one brings up the mattresses and covers.

We had barely settled in our quarters, when Kaé, completely sober by now, threw himself at the feet of the captain in an act of folly and cried out, 'Make the boat turn back! I have left my case at Vientiane!' Pitiful adventure! In his state of drunkenness, he had not thought about the transport of his case that was left behind in some corner of Vientiane with all the beautiful *sampots* in soft silk and all the coquettish apparel to fan himself like a peacock in Luang-Prabang and Bangkok. He was in despair; he pulled his hair; he wanted to return.

As consolation, a passenger promised Kaé that he would take care of his case as soon as he returned to Vientiane and would have it delivered to him in Pnom Penh in the more or less distant future. Then, we tried to convince him of the fact that he would be much better off walking through the jungle without his case.

The landscape changed by degrees. We rediscovered mountains on the horizon. The temperature also dropped. It was cold on the spar deck and I feared that the two passengers silently cursed me the following night for that old gallantry that obliged them to catch cold in the open air so that I could be lodged so comfortably. A game of bridge that reunited us in the front cabin immediately created the companionship common on boats. Then there was the first dinner together at the extreme front around a rather small table for eight diners.

After dinner, we rested at Kok Peung, the end-point of the steam-service of the *Messageries Fluviales*. From here, all year round, there are only pirogues to transport the mail, the passengers and the luggage. They use twenty to twenty-five days to cover this stretch with difficulty, up to Luang-Prabang, which we are counting on to cover in five days. The young Laotian woman from Luang-Prabang who accompanied us with her half-breed baby to Vientiane, will henceforth travel there in this way. I met her yesterday in Vientiane. She was jealous of our speedy mode of transport. But the *résident superieur* was inflexible on this issue: no local women are allowed on the *La Grandière*.

Since he belongs to the Administration and thanks to the skill of the pilot, our good boat accomplishes the feat of sailing up the river to Luang-Prabang once a year. Formerly, as a gun-boat, it had even explored the Mekong above Luang-Prabang up to the Burmese border. So much daring will perhaps cost it its life one day but nevertheless, it has motivated an enterprising businessman from Vientiane to emulate it. He has constructed a small steamer that, loaded with merchandise, has already covered the route from Vientiane to Luang-Prabang twice. The name of this little vessel, the *Malgré Tout*,[1] indicates the many obstacles her enterprising proprietor has already met with in constructing it in place, without workshops and without experienced workers and with the parts being shipped by pirogue. We believe we will cross paths, when she makes her return trip. Captain Mélan was not without anxiety about this: he feared a collision in a rapid.

As soon as we had moored, the locals of Kok Peung came aboard the spar deck and offered us, in a silver bowl (the *ô* in Laotian), the symbolic welcome gifts: first a bouquet of leaves that substitute the customary flowers that the suddenness of our arrival has not allowed the locals to gather from the forest, then candles of wax, four candles big as fingers and made out of yellow wax that embalms the wild honey taken from bee hives in the jungle. The Laotians are in effect very good at discovering and looting these nests of wild bees, and by so doing competing with the small honey-bears which one encounters from time to time in the country. They are so funny with their wide necklaces of tawny hairs contrasting with the dark coat. How could we thank the locals for their gifts? We poured a glass of rum, full to the brim, for the chief who had presided over the rites of homage. 'That's better than rice whisky,' he said. His fellow men cast him glances of envy, but, our limited provisions did not allow us to booze up the whole delegation.

12 November 1909

It was a day of rapids. Especially, the morning passed by fighting against the currents that rolled from one river-bank to the other, and in avoiding the rocks that appeared in the middle of the stream, awash with foam. Here is the Keng Ngan Kho, the Keng You and also the Keng Tiane that, in February 1905, had devoured the medical doctor who accompanied the French-Siamese border delimitation mission of Colonel Bernard. This unfortunate doctor descended the Mekong on a raft made of two pirogues tied together. Two members of the same mission, who traveled in the same way, considered it wise to leave their rafts in the hands of oarsmen for the passage of the rapids and to follow the bank on foot. Only the doctor, ill with a fit of fever, tempted his luck. The two other rafts passed without damage but his, engulfed by whirlpool, was sucked into the abyss, and disappeared with men and mice. The corpse of the doctor was found 300 meters downstream after several days of searching but never was anything seen of the oarsmen or of the raft.

It is not surprising then that these mysterious disappearances have left impressions on the naive imaginations of the Laotians who imagine the depths of a stream to be inhabited by gods and spirits that are both beneficial and fearsome. A local chief of Vientiane, nevertheless with a rather open, intelligent mind, was surprised at the sight of the *La Grandière*—that one could sail like this, without oarsmen and without oars. The mechanism of the steam-engine was explained to him; he was shown the boiler, the piston; it seemed to interest him, he assured us that he had understood it well, then, after a silence, he said: 'Yes, I see, I see! . . . But you did not tell me which is the *phy* (the spirit) that makes your boat run.'

Mountains, covered from the foothills to the top with thick vegetation, bordered the banks of the river. The stream seemed to be very narrow, the size of a stream in Europe. Sudden bends veiled its course. The morning's washing up and lunch were interrupted by incidents caused by fits of rolling, because the boat twirled

Plate 18 *A woman of Vientiane with an ô, a Laotian, silver goblet.*

Plate 19 *The gallery of sitting Buddhas in the Sisaket pagoda in Vientiane (Photo Péri).*

around and was shaken up by the bubbling waters. However, we increased the pressure; geared up for the assault and succeeded. Luckily for us, Captain Mélan knows the route very well. I complemented him, in the evening, when the boat had come to rest. 'It is not finished,' he said smiling. Never mind, we have great confidence. Captain Mélan, however, is not even a sailor by profession. He is a supervisor of Public Works, in charge of navigation on the river. He has learned to pilot boats and since by virtue of his assignment, knows the crossings better than anyone else—no-one would be more appropriate for the command of the *La Grandière.*

13 November 1909

In the morning, the boat sailed out into a stream which appeared to be like cotton wool and the thick fog embraced and hid the banks until eleven o'clock. The two passengers on the bridge were overcome by the humidity. I heard them cough deplorably above my head at night. When the sun melted the fog, we rediscovered the mountains tumbling down into the stream. Here then, the dance of the rapids started anew. Yet again we crossed over rocks. We eluded, as far as possible, the powers of the currents by zigzagging—nevertheless the boat rolled, pitched, dived and rose again as if encountering a day of bad weather. Oh! Captain Mélan will you not allow us to lunch quietly and will you not have pity on our stomachs that are driven wild by the distress of seasickness—really, seasickness, precisely! The afternoon was calm. We steamed up a reach without rapids to arrive before long at Muong Paklay, on the right hand bank of the Mekong.

Here we are then in the kingdom of Luang-Prabang, this operetta kingdom that the French Government has allowed to continue to exist in the North of Laos, perhaps as an amusement, being satisfied with asserting an active protectorate over it that provides to the commissioner, or the resident, all effective authority. In 1904, on the occasion of the convention with Siam, 500 kilometers of the right bank in which Paklay is enclosed as an enclave, and which previously formed the neutral zone, were ceded to us because they rightfully belong to the kingdom of Luang-Prabang. In Paklay, this strip of land extends into the interior over sixty kilometers to the top of the chain that forms the line of division between the valleys of the Mekong and the Menam.

We took a walk through the village. It was the first completely Laotian center that we encountered, since Vientiane and Savanaket are marked by the footprints of the Europeans that live there and the small villages that we visited on the banks are but small conglomerations of huts. There are two hundred Laotian houses here, constructed on the border of the stream or along shady avenues cut through the forest. Leaning against the vigorous and straight trunks of tropical trees, these light habitations seem to be fragile bird-cages, unsteadily balanced on their poles. Honestly, these are lively and chattering bird-like beings, the *pou sao* who risk their little impish faces in the small square openings which appear in partitions to serve as windows. Unfortunately, there are also, as prominent foreground figures, old, ape-like women, carrying their yelling babies at their breasts, while squatting on the steps of ladders.

The two whites of the country are lodged in houses that are a little bit bigger. They are the administrator and a civil servant of the Postal Services. The latter is charged with installing the telegraphic line that will link Paklay with Vientiane. The line from Vientiane to Luang-Prabang passes through the interior of the country, thus avoiding the large loop that the Mekong makes near Paklay. This

Plate 20 *In Paklay, the children stared at us with their mischievous eyes.*

implies that poor Paklay has, as news from the world, nothing other than that brought by pirogues and it lacks correspondence altogether if the postal pirogue goes down in a rapid—a rather frequent mishap. That is exactly what occurred yesterday: the mail pirogue capsized not far from Paklay. The consequences for Upper Laos are that official and private correspondence of fifteen days have been destroyed and one local oarsman has drowned.

We dined on the spar deck. The moon, in her first quarter, was only a fine inlay of silver against a sky of lapis lazuli, which curiously bent towards the small boat where good conversation, exclamations of unusually happy moods, fused into this dreamy serenity of the stream by which I gradually felt impregnated . . . . I would have liked to communicate with wild nature, listen to dark language and, to understand her—become like these simple people of this country . . . . I sat down by the railing, a little distance away from my companions, and lost myself in dreams that floated from one bank to the other, remaining there a long time, but a far away voice tore me away from my solitude.

It was a passenger narrating a story about Laos: the re-enactment of a crime invented by a pompous administrator. 'When the guilty person had been found,' said the story-teller, 'the administrator wanted to confront him with his victim to create an impact on his soul and nerves. But, since the victim had been buried for

41

several days, he decided to use a willing soldier as a substitute. He put him to sleep on the ground, on the very spot and in the same condition in which the corpse had been discovered. He then spread around his head the contents of a box of concentrated milk, to represent the brain, and sprayed his whole body with a bottle of red ink . . . the spilled blood! The mosquito's, attracted by the sweetened milk, tickled the forehead of the soldier who could not remain as still as a corpse and the murderer, not at all affected, offered only vivid denials at the administrator's question: 'Do you recognize the victim?' The whole village, which was present at the scene, was overtaken by cheerfulness, the supposed corpse and the accused joined in, only the poor administrator, far from laughing, cursed and swore, furious with the lack of success of his contrivance.

It is, however, not untrue that one can easily bluff the naive Laotians. The subterfuge that one ascribes to an old commissioner of Laos, the most spiritual of the representatives of France in Indochina, clearly illustrates this. Going on tour, he asked the notables of a province to come to him and, while with them, he solemnly dropped his glass eye into a decanter of water—because he was a one-eyed man—saying to them: 'I'm leaving, but I leave you my eye. By it, I will continue to watch over you!' The fear for this fetish eye was sufficient to preserve respect in the province.

Another incident proves very well the gullibility of the Laotians; gullibility that, this time, had catastrophic consequences for them. Some years ago, to the East of Savanaket, the locals mounted an uprising against the local police, an agitator having assured them that in case of repression the bullets of the French would convert themselves into almond flowers. The confidence of these unfortunate revolutionaries did not last beyond the first volley of bullets that wounded some of them. Moreover, it was the only revolt that had to be suppressed since the beginning of the French occupation. The Laotians are very happy under our guardianship which they long awaited as a safeguard against the successive incursions of the Siamese and the Chinese from Yunnan.

14 November 1909

We left Paklay at 7 a.m., taking with us the administrator. Again this damned fog rendered an uncertainty in navigation and that went to the hearts of the passengers! All took refuge in the cabin in front, idle because the usual distractions were missing: one could not see the banks, which resulted in disappointments for those who were content with observing the scenery, and an even greater disappointment for the hunters who habitually exercised their skills on flocks of peacocks. That morning then, books became the only saviour from boredom: some volumes of Kipling had been appropriated from the small library in Vientiane. To read them in a country so alike the Indian jungle described by the author, in the company of people who have often lived the lives of heroes in these tales, was to increase our savouring them tenfold.

Like yesterday, the fog dissipated by 11 a.m. when we stopped for our supply of firewood. In front of us, on the left bank, an enormous, superb rock dominated us and its smooth flank, which the sun starkly lit, fell vertically into the stream. On the bank that we accosted, some locals roamed about idly with an air of indifference on the outskirts of a small village, the huts of which were almost all in ruins. I entered one of these huts. No cries of children, no grunting of the pigs that are so dear in Indochina. It's desolation; it's death. Three years ago, an epidemic of cholera had decimated the village. Most of the survivors had fled and the victorious jungle embraced the ruined huts.

During lunch some collisions of the plates prepared us for the emotions of the afternoon. At 3 p.m., in the middle of a game of bridge for which no-one mustered any passion, a violent shock came to us. This was followed by a cracking that immobilized us on a rock, we ran aground. Maybe it is the end of the trip! A second of silence, of anguish, then it was the pandemonium that such an adventure brings aboard: the ringing of bells, appeals, orders hurled across at the stokers. The engine spat, the steel plates shuddered, we tried to sail backwards before the traitorous rock could reassure its grip . . . . Hurrah! The boat disengaged herself. She disengaged so well that we sailed backwards a hundred meters at full speed. Quickly to the holds! They were dry, all is well. A jolt at the helm and we restarted the painful march by trial and error, the slow and patient fight against the current, the assault on the whirlpools, the flight for the reefs.

During the course of the entire day, the bed of the Mekong was so narrow, and the mountains veiled by tall black forests projected so much shadow on the bends and roundabouts, before us, to the right, and to the left, that the water appeared dark and grim like an infernal stream. The wild appearance of the landscape was oppressing. If only the sun had brought us some light for a few hours today.

Plate 21 *Elephants in the jungle near Vientiane.*

We searched for a quiet loop to pass the night and found a sandy bank at the edge of the river. We tied up the boat. On the sand, fresh tracks of tigers and panthers mixed with those of peacocks, the fine hoofs of does, the turned-back claws of monkeys and the soft furrows of reptiles. These guests of the forest came to drink at the Mekong last night, under the light of the moon. While we sleep, they will come back, smothered foot steps, contemplating this big, unknown machine that is our boat. The ferocious beasts will smell the living flesh protected against their lusts by the flanks of the *La Grandière*. I will dream of tigers and panthers all night long, because they have talked about them all evening. That is, if I am not woken up by the noises of a fight, as it sometimes happens between tigers and elephants, in the depths of the forest. I have heard about a tame elephant called Cleo, who was made to work in the exploitation of wood on an island of the Lower Mekong. She fought a frightful struggle against a tiger one night. We are no longer in 'the times when the animals could talk' and the brave animal has not recounted her feat. Only in the morning, when Cleo regained her place of work, her feet were stained with the blood of another beast, and a bit farther, lay a dead tiger, that had been crushed under the weight of the pachyderm.

The tiger is a neighbor to be feared, here like anywhere else in Indochina, boldly searching for its prey even in villages. When the night arrives, the inhabitants have every reason to fear from him. The *colon* of a village in the interior heard the terrified neighing of his horse late one evening. He ran to the stable accompanied by a coolie and his local wife, who, while providing light, also carried their child in her arms. The light was dim. He did not see his horse in the box, extended his hand and encountered a warm fur. The woman brought the lamp nearer: a tiger was seated astride the horse lapping up blood. The coolie disappeared with a leap into the jungle, the woman, crying out, dropped the lamp and the child to run faster and the *colon*, shuddering with fear, groped for the child in the dark and steathily slunk away. When he returned with a gun, the beast had gone.

Thus, the strongest feelings and the greatest affections will stop in the face of the fright inspired by this terrible and deceitful guest. The obsessive fear of the tiger results in acts of cowardice brought on by the survival instinct. Witness the adventure of this European who was passing through a village in Laos and who shared the mat of a shy, little Laotian woman. The night was hot, and he positioned himself as close as possible to the door to get some air, in a straw hut, the floor of which was almost level with the soil. Suddenly, he was awakened by the strong, warm breath of an animal on his face. 'The tiger,' he shouted, upright at once. He brutally lifted his companion who was sleeping peacefully against the wall, deposited her as a sacrifice under the breath of the monster and . . . .took off through the window. A peal of laughter from the *pou sao* rang out and halted his flight. He learned midway through the jibe that this tiger was a well meaning buffalo who, prowling about around the hut, wanted to pay them a visit.

15 November 1909

A superb day! The valley narrowed further, the mountains rose in terraces around us. Enormous rock formations, detached from the flanks of these mountains divert and break the waters, if they cannot ride over them. With each turn, we found the mountains transformed, the rocks formed other pitfalls. Our route seemed to be blocked in this way at every moment like a dead end wall from which the stream seemed to emerge.

At 10 a.m., we met the *Malgré Tout* in a passage that luckily was large enough to avoid a collision. The vessel saluted the *La Grandière* and hurtled down at fifty kilometers an hour, while we had so much trouble to ascending! She then appeared to us like a wisp of straw taken in the direction of the maze of rocks. Then, a turn took her away from our vision. At noon, we boarded wood in a hamlet, the inhabitants of which offered us the usual gifts. Renewal of the scene in Kok Peung: the leaves and the candles presented in an *ô* and the libations of rum offered by us to the notable, a beautiful Laotian with a soft and fun-loving look.

The cook needed to buy supplies. I assisted in the sacrifice of an unlucky suckling-pig and in an amusing chase, or rather, the capture of some chickens. In this country, the fowl is so wild and carefree that it is impossible for housewives to catch it by hand. Well then, one spreads out some grain under the hut, between the struts that support it, and from the interior of the house, as soon as the chicken approaches, one lassoes it.

After lunch, we entered a big rapid, the Keng Luong. The jolted boat was inundated with foam. Captain Mélan forbade us to climb on the spar deck as long as the equilibrium was unstable. In the cupboard, the plates were clanging against each other. We heard the boat groan and the boiler blow. The bumps threw us like inert objects on the seats of the front cabin. Nothing escaped from being banged

Plate 22 *By raft in a rapid. Enormous outcrops of rocks, detached from the sides of the mountain, deviate and break the float.*

about in the boiling mass of the waters. One had the urge to ask for mercy, to shout: enough, as in a series of roller-coaster or swinging that has lasted too long . . .

Towards the end of the day, in Tha Dua, we stopped again to take in wood. That was our first encounter with the troops of His Majesty Sisavong, the king of Luang-Prabang. There were some soldiers of his special guard here, smartly dressed in deep blue, with a kind of small, alpine beret as headgear. They exercised seriously on the bank. Upon our arrival, the corporal commanded: 'Present the guns.' In his haste, he forgot to turn his small detachment around to face the stream so that these soldiers presented their backs to the *La Grandière* and their guns to the mountains. It does not matter, they are gallant, these small soldiers of Sisavong. All our compliments, Sire!

Plate 23 *Sleeping Buddha at the hall of festivities in Vientiane (Photo Péri).*

Chapter 3

Luang-Prabang

Some Laotian history—The economic future of Laos—The dances of the Khas and the moon nights in Luang-Prabang—The market—Laotian customs—The elephants on a walk—King Sisavong and his court—A king who regrets Paris—A small, shy princess—Pirogue races—Laotian orchestra's—The pagodas and the monks—The Buddha's footprint—Burmese merchandise—A visit to the queen mother—The Na Luang farm—Laotian theater—The royal procession in That Luang—The folk-festivities of the twelfth month—A Franco-Laotian supper—Departure from Luang-Prabang—The descend of the Mekong—The wrecking of the La Grandière

We now come to the period in my travelogue when we will be acquainted with the kingdom of Luang-Prabang, the most interesting region of Laos, and the principal motivation for my embarking on this trip. Before I talk about the festivities that we await, I think that I should give, in a nut shell, a description of Laos in general and the kingdom of Luang-Prabang in particular.

One can say that the Laotian countries occupy the whole basin of the Mekong, comprised between Cambodia, down stream, and Burma, up stream, i.e., that it stretches over 1,200 kilometers.

The French protectorate extends over the basin of the left bank and also over two territories on the right bank, one in the South: the provinces of Bassac and Malouprey (Cambodian border), the other in the North: the territories of Paklay forming part of the Kingdom of Luang-Prabang. Everywhere else, the Mekong is the limit that separates French Laos from Siamese Laos.

Plate 24 *Kha orchestra. These are hollow bamboo sticks of various sizes.*

French Laos is approximately as large as Siamese Laos, however, its population is only 500,000 inhabitants, compared to the three million in Siamese Laos. This difference is without doubt due to the fact that the regions of the right bank are more mountainous than those of the left bank.[1] The difference is also due to the systematic depopulation of the left bank to the benefit of the right bank, implemented by the Siamese during the last century. It goes without saying that the figures that I provide here, are only approximations.

The population of Laos is composed almost exclusively of Laotians *sensu strictu* and of Khas. The Laotians are a Thai race. The Thais, with origins in the Southeast of China, have settled in the distant past in the valleys of Laos and Siam. The Khas are considered the aborigines of Laos. These fetishist savages, of a type completely different to the Laotians, live more or less independent lives in the mountains, with their own customs and traditions.

Laos had been divided over many centuries into a great number of little kingdoms and Luang-Prabang was one of the most important. These kingdoms, instead of uniting among themselves, constantly battled with each other, thereby allowing their powerful neighbors to subjugate them on several occasions. They first underwent the domination of the Khmers, the masters of Cambodia; then West-Laos was incorporated into the kingdom of Pegu until the year 1225; later still, in the sixteenth century, another part of Laos, the right bank of the Mekong, was conquered by the Siamese.

In the seventeenth century, the kingdom of Luang-Prabang was successively invaded by the Burmese and by the Annamites. However, it was especially in the last century that this country was overwhelmed by fate. In 1828, when the Siamese crossed the Mekong, destroyed Vientiane—the rival of Luang-Prabang and sometime its vassal—Luang-Prabang, to avoid the same fate and hoping to be protected by the Siamese from Haw Chinese looters, offered to pay tribute to Bangkok, while continuing to pay tribute to Annam and even to China. That did not, however, stop the 'yellow flags' from ravaging the East of the kingdom in 1875. The Siamese who were approached for help, managed to finish the work of the Chinese pirates, holding to ransom and depopulating the country of Luang-Prabang, where they installed a commissioner and a Siamese garrison. From there, they made incursions into neighboring countries and even into Tonkin. As a consequence, Luang-Prabang had to undergo, in 1887, retaliations for the looting done by the Siamese in the Black River—the Tonkinese set the city ablaze, with little resistance, that had been abandoned by the Siamese without struggle. The old Laotian king and his unfortunate subjects at once fled up to Paklay in pirogues, many of which sunk at the passage of the rapids.

It is natural, after so many adventures, that the Laotians have voluntarily accepted the establishment of a French protectorate in their country. Moreover, our explorers had already obtained the sympathy of the population. The first of these men was the naturalist Mouhout (from 1858 until 1861).

After Mouhout, Luang-Prabang was visited by the mission of Doudart de Lagrée that followed the route of the Mekong (1866 until 1868). Finally, years later, Mr. Pavie and his collaborators accomplished in these territories of Laos the marvelous work of penetration, and as a result of this in 1893, the protectorate was established on the grounds of France's right to claim the secular suzerainty of Annam over Laos. That was not accomplished without meeting with strong resistance from the Siamese, the incursions of which on the left bank of the Mekong had partly served as a goal to be able to attribute the right of the first occupant. One had to deploy French troops on the Mekong and at the same time stage a naval demonstration in Bangkok.

The treaty of 1893, by giving us the left bank of the Mekong, had created a neutral zone twenty-five kilometers wide on the right bank. The treaty of 1904 canceled this zone and gave us on the right bank two territories that I have already cited above.

Of the old kingdoms of Laos, only Luang-Prabang is still left. Her king has limited attributions that he shares with the *Senak* or the council of notables.

From the economic angle, Laos is not devoid of natural resources. Mr. Doumer had called it the agricultural, forest and mine reserve of Indochina. On the Laotian slopes of the Annamite chain, one finds, together with the gold about which I have already talked, lead, tin and copper. Iron and coal are also found there. Agricultural life is especially developed in the middle Mekong, towards Savanaket, where there is a vast plain of rice paddy and cows and buffalo-rearing. The forests of Upper Laos contain precious wood and especially a lot of teak. In Laos, we can also find benzoin, cardamom, and lac. Finally, cotton is cultivated, which, like in Cambodia, is very good and very silky, but the local method of shelling is

Plate 25 *A street in Luang-Prabang (Photo Sesmaisons).*

In Laos and Siam

Plate 26 *Kha women. They are wearing the sine, a Laotian dress, small jackets and high bonnets of rolled-up cloths.*

Plate 27 *A dance of Kha women.*

defective in both countries and the cotton, being imperfectly separated from the shell, is almost impossible to use in the mills of Europe.

Thanks to the Khas who are employed as lumberjacks, the exploitation of teak, which can be rather easily floated on the Mekong in the right season, has been started. It would be very beneficial if this business could be further developed because the teak of Burma and Siam is becoming rare as a result of unplanned exploitation and the teak of Java, that is now on offer in the European markets seems to be of a quality quite inferior to that of Indochina.

Unfortunately, apart from rice culture, livestock-rearing, cutting teak and dredging for gold, the exploitation of the resources of Laos is nil, due to lack of workers, and especially transportation routes.

The Khas, who only work in the forests, have potential as coolies if one could succeed in taming their savagery. Regarding the Laotians, they do not know anything other than sailing pirogues. You should not count on employing them for work because they are lazy to the extreme—centuries of oppression have killed all energies in them. Moreover, they have few needs and seldom dream about savings. Among them, there are no artists, except for the builders of pirogues. Luckily, the Annamites quite easily settle in Laos. It is they who monopolize the professions of carpenter, mason, and baker. The Europeans are even obliged to rely on them for domestic help.

The creation of communication routes is evidently a question of money. One has renounced linking Laos with Tonkin by a railway line. However, the administration has studied two projects for railways up to Vientiane: one from Savanaket to Quantri (Annam), the other from Compong-Tiam (Cambodia) to Savanaket, going around the Kemmarat rapids by the right bank of the Mekong. This last line would be less expensive than the first. Nevertheless, one estimates an expense amounting to 25 million French francs.

A service between Vientiane and Luang-Prabang would only function for part of the year—assuming that a public steam navigation service is infact established. Also, the administration plans the construction of a route into the interior that would link Luang-Prabang with the navigable reach of the Middle-Mekong and with the planned railway lines.

Plate 28 *Luang-Prabang girls. They are adorned with necklaces, bracelets and ear-rings in gold from Laos. A gold chain is rolled around the bun.*

All these communication lines need to be established urgently. Our occupation has provided Laos with a security that it has never known before. Now we are left with the obligation of drawing it out of its isolation and making it participate in the economic development of other countries of Indochina.

16 November 1909

As soon as we approached Luang-Prabang, the valley widened. At the same time the landscape brightened up and the presence of man manifests itself. On the hillsides, large spaces that have been denuded by fire, are used for upland rice cultivation. We passed pirogues decorated with flowers and with banners and loaded with passengers who sang and conversed gaily. Everyone went to Luang-Prabang for the festivities. We arrived there at 2 p.m. and our *La Grandière* moored at the foot of a stone staircase, higher than twenty meters which the stream hides during high waters, but which is, today, almost completely in the open.

I believe that all of the Europeans of Luang-Prabang awaited our landing. It was the distraction of the day. They had calculated the hour of our arrival, in case the rapids would let us pass, and to receive us, we saw but smiles of welcome, hands offered, words of greeting. They escorted us along an avenue with trees bordering the stream, then into a larger cross-street, which seemed to me to be the main street of Luang-Prabang. But what a strange street for a capital city! It's more like a path through a park, bordered by flowering Japanese lilac trees which veiled, with their purple bunches, the rickety houses in bamboo and the wooden temples with their pointed roofs.

We first stopped in the garden, under some sort of kiosk, very *couleur locale*, pompously called: European Club. An amiable speech by the commissioner of the Government, Mr. Grand, champagne in our glasses and we celebrated the success of our journey. Then, the French shared the burden of lodging all of us. We followed Mr. Grand who had prepared a small apartment for us at the *commissariat*, a large old wooden house in the middle of the avenue with the Japanese lilac trees. It transpired that the wood-lice eat away at the joists of this house, that the snakes make their nests in the beams of the ceiling but the structure was hugged closely by a marvelous garden full of shade, scents, flapping wings and bird-song. Two old Chinese statues in granite, representing I do not know what blissfully happy spirits, stand guard at the foot of the terrace that precedes the reception hall of the *commissariat* and under the golden sun of this Laotian autumn, the house seems to radiate entirely with the optimistic peace of mind transfixed in the smile of these Chinese maggots.

It will do us good to stop here . . . Our servants brought, with great trouble, our luggage since one could not count during those days on the people of the land offering any help whatsoever. All were resting. There were no more coolies. There were only people celebrating the festivities who walked about and sang, draping brilliant cotton dresses over their shoulders, tickling the *pou sao* who burst out laughing. In short, the most miserable Laotians of Luang-Prabang despised working today and cared little for futile profits. What good is hard work! It's the celebration. The sky was without clouds and tonight, the songs, the games, the smiling flirtations will take place as a sacred ritual under the clearness of the propitious moon—of the moon who is the true goddess of Luang-Prabang because the ancient Tanitus of Egypt[2] seems to be revived here in a new cult of love and grace, with the entire population as priests and priestesses to serve it.

In spite of the mildness of the temperature, many young boys had thrown brightly coloured cotton covers over their heads and shoulders. The reason is that the cover is for a young man, for a *pou bao* as one says in Laotian, an elegant piece of clothing. If he possesses one, it replaces all the other garments for the upper part of the body. With a rainbow-colored cover and with artistic tattoos he can hope to conquer many hearts.

From our first outing, our sympathies were with these happy locals who placed themselves along the edges of the roads, and bowed to the ground to greet us, at the same time respectful and cheerful, as our carriage passed by. We traveled in the carriage of the commissioner—a luxury that has arrived here how I know not—and Mr. Grand introduced us to the sights. This city, built up around a peak, the Pou Si, on which there is a *that*, is still a flowering forest in which the houses resemble the nests of birds—a forest only a little more denuded than the big virgin forest that covers the nearby mountains.

Oh! What a delightful paradise of a *far niente* this country protects, by the fierce barrier of the stream, against progress and ambitions for which it has no need! Will Luang-Prabang be, in our century of exact sciences, of quick profits, of

Plate 29 *Two young Lao women.*

victory by money, the refuge of the last dreamers, the last loved ones, the last troubadours? It is in reality a love, a dream, a poetry of naive sensuality which enfolds under the foliage of this perfumed forest. We perceived it from the first evening.

After dinner, which reunited all the passengers of the *La Grandière*, a kha orchestra could be heard in the garden of the *commissariat*. We went to see these khas, savages that are rather gentile if one does not offend their customs, or their superstitions, but, their appearance is rather fierce because of their long shaggy hair—almost their only piece of clothing—which covers them sometimes down to the loins. The women wear a *sine*, the dress of Laos, little short vests protect their breast and their hair which is braided close to the ears and held in place by a cap fashioned out of rolled up cloth.

The orchestra was very primitive: it consisted of bamboo sticks of different widths, cut in such a way that it suffices hitting the ground with them to generate sounds that are not very different from each other. At a vivid beat, one or two couples danced rhythmically—a sensual, passionate, lustful dance to the extreme. The couples turned around, approached each other, separated, their arms above their stern and savage faces, until the lasciviousness exhausted the panting dancers and musicians.

The khas distanced themselves . . . But there, in the obscurity, a strident cry resounded, a cry that was swelled and modulated seemingly reuniting a thousand cries from the North, the South, from all directions at the same time. Moan, lament, prayer, it was the appeal of the *pou sao*, the young girls, who invoked the moon and its light—accomplices of the games of love. And the *pou bao*, the young men, guided by this cry to assemble, sped to the *Cours d'Amour*, established in the squares near the wats, where the young girls, arranged in a circle, awaited their lovers. The latter placed themselves in front of the girls. They veiled themselves with their cotton fabrics and the poems developed on the lips of the improvisers of the two sexes—chants of tenderness, supplications and praise of the amorous *pou bao*, emphatic replies, biting refusals, vague promises, fine coquetries of the solicited *pou sao*. All around the spectators of this gracious duel applauded the love chants, the tender poems, the skillful propositions. Thus the hours passed in the pale light . . . The cry, overhanging over the city, very late tonight, has disturbed our sleep.

17 November 1909

The morning distraction in Luang-Prabang was a walk in the market that was installed all along the avenue not far from the Club. The elegant ladies gathered there, their breasts lightly veiled with the shawls of transparent silk in soft colours, their hips tightly fastened by a dress with large stripes that they attach below the navel. They carry, suspended by a ribbon from their shoulders the small basket of lacquer ware bamboo, the *kasa*, which is made for them by the monks of the pagodas. How coquettish it is, this national basket! So fine, so light, so well varnished that one would not dare to put fruits in it, nor flowers of lianas or orchids, resembling frail and shiny insects which would mix later adorn the soft hair, or form necklaces.

But, at the stalls of the small traders, squatting under large umbrellas imported from Europe, several other products found a place next to the flowers. There was poultry and pieces of rare pork. There were fried grasshoppers on sticks and all sorts of big insects which comprise the delicacies of Laotian gourmet. Then, enormous fishes from the Mekong, basketsfull of small, brown rice from the mountains, mounds of salt, herbs, and as in all the markets of Indochina, heaps of areca nuts, betel leaves and the pink, crushed lime which produces the inevitable betel-chew inflicting on the natives that black mouth, so visually disagreeable.

In little barracks, established in their homes, other merchants displayed imported products which the caravans, that came from Siam or Burma, have poured out over Luang-Prabang: cotton fabrics, blankets, pieces of silk, shawls, cotton velvet, haberdashery and stripes of tinsel, all the poor-quality stuff that should seduce these primitives. Alas! Almost all these things had English and German factory labels and they were supplied by houses of these nationalities, established in Bangkok. Very little French merchandise arrives here, be it by the dangerous route of the Mekong, or by the sparse convoys from Tonkin which follow the Black River, then cross by the trail through North-East Laos. Aren't there any faster and less dangerous routes of transport to Tonkin and Annam to compete with foreign businesses and thereby make the people from Luang-Prabang surrender their dependence on the Siamese caravans!

For the moment, we can only oppose an increase in the customs duties related to this influx of foreign goods. That is for me the indirect cause of deception. I would

Plate 30 *A pirogue loaded with musicians and actors on their way to the festivities (Photo Berger).*

have loved to bring along as a souvenir of my journey, some hides of flying squirrels which come from Burma—a beautiful fine fur resembling that of a silver-fox. Formerly, these hides were easy to find in Luang-Prabang, but, it was in vain that I searched the displays of the shops. The caravans do not bring them anymore since they have been hit by high duties.

By 9 a.m. the animation in the market-place reached its peak. Today it was more gay than usual, without doubt because of the festivities which have emptied the huts. They shouted, laughed, sang. The young girls glided by gracefully, holding back their shawls which were unwound by the wind, with one hand. Heavy gold jewels jingled on the wrists and necks of women, their costumes in warm hues sparkled under the harsh light and in the air, the odor of dying flowers, of sticks of sandal wood and of sweaty skins hung about sensually.

The boys, painted bright saffron by their mothers and nude as small Saint-Johns, ran between the legs of the strolling people, jumped boldly on top of the baskets of the merchants and fell into the piles of rice and salt. The very small ones cried on the breasts of their grandmothers', horrible old women, who, well out of line, found it unnecessary to hide their wrinkled flesh under the shawls that young women wear. Oh! horrible display of nudity, offered without remorse by these hideous female monkeys with their coarse, gray, crew cut hairdos! They nevertheless smiled friendly, showing their blackened teeth behind lips bleeding with pink lime, which the betel gnaws at and deforms.

These nudes, so little preserved by the rays of tropical sunshine called to mind the phrase that one attributes to an old resident of Laos. He was upset because a French woman found the Laotian women too brown: 'Under their *sines*, madam, they are as white as you and me.' It is very well possible for the skin of the old colonial servants, but, the lady must have been little flattered to serve this comparison as well.

Even though six to eight European woman have already visited Luang-Prabang since the French occupation, I enjoyed great success as a object of good willed curiosity among the Laotian women, young and old. Sao Toug Di, Sao Bang, Sao Thane, Sao Khay, all the *sao* surrounded me. They discreetly caressed my hands and, my clothes. Laughs burst from their lips and their grace like young cats increased my regret at not being able to answer to their babbling and to their compliments in their language.

The extreme liberty of morals that reign here make foreigners easily find the hospitality that one ascribes to Scotland: one readily compares Luang-Prabang with the fatherland of Rarahu, and refers to it as the Tahiti of Indochina. One must take into account though not to upset the spirits of the ancestors, but, since libations and ritual gifts appease them, the young girls are seldom shy. We met numerous widows who had certainly been consoled. Some have kept the most notable name of one of their occasional husbands. Here is, for example, Princess X, which one names after a royal explorer who has honoured her, some years ago. The pseudo-princess is not very young anymore, her charm has withered and I must admit that nothing august brings her to attention.[3]

This same liberty of morals permits the Europeans who live in Laos to set up real local families. If I belief the stories which I have heard some echoes of, this custom is rather detrimental to some who, being unable to instill the habits and tastes of the West in these local women, themselves become imperceptibly real Laotians, lost for the role of civilizer which they could have filled. Others detach themselves and leave forever their children when the necessities of their careers oblige them to do so. What a pity to abandon them to these women who can only make Laotians out of them!

Plate 31 *A group of Meo men and women, a Laotian people of Chinese origins.*

To remedy this state of affairs, it is obviously necessary that the young Frenchmen of Laos marry French women. But how many of them would dare to ask a *fiancé* to start a family in Laos! The young girls of France, less adventurous than the English girls, would be scared of the life that awaits them here. And thus it is a great pity for morality in general. So much abuse of all kinds is caused by the influence that the Laotian women exercise in the end over the European . . . .which diminishes considerably—one can conceive of it—the prestige of French authority.

In the market we met our wild people, the khas, of yesterday again. We also made the acquaintance of another variety of wild men, the Meos, of which the slanting eyes and locks of tied hair, for the men on the top of their heads, reminded us of their Chinese origins. Khas, Meos and Laotians of the plains filled the street, bartered the products of the land with the Burmese: tea, benzoin, rubber, and lac, for goods brought by the caravans. One could hardly get around. Then, suddenly, the crowd stepped aside, dispersed, leaving a wide road empty in the middle of which only some sniveling babies were left to demand their mothers' attention by crying loudly. This was because from the court yard of the Royal Palace which opens smack in the middle of the market, the elephants of the king, in a group guided by mahouts, arrived. They invaded the street, swishing their trunks along, shaking their large ears, formidable animals on their enormous limbs. There were first the children of the mamas—elephants that advanced on nimble limbs, each carrying a boy heaved upon their necks. Then came the adult elephants, humorous with irony in their little, lively eyes. The subjects of Sisavong are accustomed to these strolls of domesticated elephants, which are as inoffensive as our cows in France. They only preoccupy themselves with stacking away bunches of bananas from the searching trunks of the big animals that devour them and which they lift up skillfully amidst the laughter of the people. Thus, the group strolled about, making the ground shudder under their heavy feet. After them, the crowd closed in and soon one saw them no more, except for the conductors of the elephants, who, high up on the backs, swayed, rolled, reeled which each step, thus dominating the circle of onlookers . . .

In the afternoon, as a prelude to the festivities, there were pirogue races on the Mekong. We passed through the same gateway in the royal quarters which the elephants have crossed this morning. Then we followed the crowd which passed before the great cabin of the king and which then took its place in the elevated stands built on the edge of the stream for the occasion. Places had been reserved for us in the official stand which had been lined with cotton fabric in lively colors. We had barely arrived when King Sisavong, at the sharp and noise tones of an orchestra, appeared, on a gilded throne carried by men. His guards escorted him; these were the same soldiers that had saluted us in Tha Dua in costumes of Alpine hunters. But, today they were in parade uniforms. Their whole attire was white, including the beret, so that they looked like kitchen boys. We were looking for the spit which must be the weapon of these warriors of the third Thursday in Lent.

His Majesty descended from the throne. He is a young man of twenty-eight years, smiling and kind. His face, a bit bloated, is very pale, his skin is almost white. Initial signs of portliness do not detract from his natural dignity. He was dressed in a deep green *sampot* and a damask jacket, embroidered with heavy gold arabesques. Servants relieved him of his elongated tiara and, after the presentations, he sat at the edge of the stand and offered me a chair to his right. One had told me: 'In any case, always take a place on the same row as the king: to seat oneself in front of someone, in the code of Laotian etiquette, is to accept for oneself inferiority and servitude.' I had not followed this advice: the friendly, little king is too familiar with our customs to attach any significance to this Laotian custom when in the presence of Frenchmen.

Sisavong was, in effect, for some time, a Parisian in Paris. Although he was the son of the old Sacharine, the preceding sovereign of Luang-Prabang, it didn't look like the order of succession to the throne would ever allow him to ascend it, and instead of giving him a completely Laotian education, he was sent, on two occasions, to attend as a student, courses at the Colonial School in Paris. There are bad mouths who pretend to know that on several occasions, in the company of fun-loving colonial officials, he savoured and appreciated the distractions of the Quartier Latin, without being bothered by any protocol. Then, the passing away of his parents had called upon him to succeed Sacharine. Finished were the joys of being a student! He returned to Luang-Prabang, made the obligatory retreat as a monk in the monastery that we now see on the right side of the stream, in the hollow of the mountain, married first three or four women, then some more this year and, has become a real Laotian again and a very worthy sovereign too of his little country.

That this sojourn in France has not left him skeptical about his rights, his duties and the importance of his role, I would not swear to when I see the mocking good-

In Laos and Siam

Plate 32 *The elephants of the King of Luang-Prabang in the market. The Laotians are accustomed to walkabouts of these domesticated elephants, as harmless as our cows in France.*

68

natured smirk which marks his lips. But what does it matter! If his role, a bit faded, is in effect that of a bone idle king, he is no less the guardian of traditions which it would be a pity to see disappear. The French Government provides him with an allowance of some forty thousand franc; there are elephants, women. He is happy, without the worry about a revolution or an anarchist bomb by which his 'cousins' in Europe are threatened. He told me nevertheless, in very pure French, that he often regrets having left Paris.

On this theme, the conversation continued between us, in front of the grand, distracted dignitaries who did not understand our language. There was the second, third, fourth king . . . How many kings! The last two were but insignificant governors of provinces. But the second king, a small Laotian of a ripe age, with an energetic and intelligent disposition—although he has never left Indochina and speaks only his mother-tongue—has been able to play an important part in the governing of the country and is very much interested in things European. Moreover, he draws with taste and promised us to sketch an itinerary for the route between Paklay and Uttaradit which he has traveled several times. Then, he installed himself in the back of the stand and began a game of chess which was not even interrupted by the feats of the rowers.

Divided into teams of twenty to thirty rowers, they sailed at full speed on long pirogues charged to the upper edge. From time to time, a boat capsized, the hull overturned completely. Under the ironic cheering of the spectators, the oarsmen, after a dive, returned to the surface, straightened the pirogue and continued the race without further mishaps. The people of Luang-Prabang are, in effect, the most agile conductors of the pirogues on the Mekong. A team, distinctively clad in red shawls, was the special team of the king. I was assured that it had obtained the first prize. I congratulated the king, without being able to say whether justice alone had designated the rewards, because, much more than the races, the decor and the strangeness of the persons that surround me captured my interest. Of special interest was the profound respect His Majesty had for a very old monk, bent and wrinkled, bony and morose. He intrigued me very much. However, I threw only furtive glances in his direction for fear of causing him distress because the monks must avoid eye contact and the company of women. He was the grand priest of the place, the pope of all the monks in the kingdom, the one that consecrated the king himself.

Plate 33 *Divided in teams of twenty to thirty oarsmen, the Laotians go at top speed in long pirogues, charged to just above the water.*

Furthermore, if I can believe the chronicles, one day he officiated as a catholic priest, solicited by a somewhat imbalanced European. The latter lived in Luang-Prabang with his wife and had just had a son. He wanted to make the grand priest baptize his son and taught him the necessary rituals . . . . The old king Sacharine, chosen as the godfather, had pondered for eight days to find a Laotian name for the baby, consisting of at least two lines, which would hold promise for all possible happiness. The father, proud of his offspring, the king, and the local musicians went in a procession to the temple. It was a memorable ceremony . . . The poor baby was not embarrassed long by his name. He died when descending the Mekong. Was it on the occasion of this christening that young boys without respect completely intoxicated the grand priest with chartreuse liquor—'a saintly liquor', they told him, 'made by your colleagues in France'? He got a taste for it, took the whole bottle and the bad jokers left him for the night, on the sofa of the *commissariat*. His sleep was so agitated that his feet spoiled the silk cover of the armchair. In the morning, he was still squatted in Laotian fashion and very sick in the middle of the torn cover and the bent springs.

That day his old face contrasted with the beauty of his neighbour, a young princess, a sister of the king, a girl of about ten years of age, fine, distinguished, with discreet manners—certainly the most exquisite doll that I have ever seen. We would all like to photograph this little, studied face, crowned by

70

a bun, set with gold chains, well balanced on top of her head, as is the custom for children. A *sine* and drapery of the same brocade as her royal brother adorned her to the neck, her wrists and her frail ankles were crushed under, murdered by the weight of the gold jewelry, so heavy that the poor girl evoked pity. She had not forgotten to adorn her ears with strange ornaments, resembling small children's trumpets, which pierce the lobes of all female ears here and elongate them, deforming them in a deplorable manner. We intimidated her greatly, but, conscientious of her dignity, she dared not show it, this little wild bird, though her hand trembled in mine.

The people moved behind our railing around the musicians that squatted in front of their instruments. They are bizarre instruments of the Laotian orchestra. Some are composed of long pieces of wood in the form of a boat, covered with keys which one hits with a small mallet; others are in a circular form. In the middle of this strange key-board the artist hits with his hammer in all directions, even behind him, with an amusing speed. This produces a sharp and dry, kitsch music, which sounds rather like an old cracked harpsichord. How much more pleasurable are the plaintiff sounds of the *khêne* which we heard in Ban Huai Kina! But, as it is, this orchestra blends well with the gaiety of the people in the festivities, with the laughing of women, with the cries of the children, with the popular chants which, leaving one person's lips, are picked up by many in chorus—always passionate and, it seems, realistic too.

Then, the last pirogue had disappeared. The king, followed by his entourage, stood up, and left the platform to approach the throne. Instantly, in the flicker of an eye, the swarming people, just a moment ago so busy, stuck their noses into the sand to honour the sovereign to which a crawling guard had presented the sparkling, pointed tiara. Sisavong stepped on the throne. He really is most composed, but he throws us the same ironic smile which we had noticed when he arrived . . . .

The carriage of Mr. Grand brought me to the *commissariat* where the civil servants of Luang-Prabang were invited to have dinner with us. They arrived successively: the inspector of the militia, the receiver of the postal department, the employee of customs, the assistants of the civil service, attached to Mr. Grand, and even a woman, the wife of an official. But she was not an European, she was a small Annamite woman, married in the presence of the mayor and the priest during a recent journey to France. In this way, the official elevated her, from being the mother of a brood of young half-castes to his legitimate wife and, be it well understood, madam has quickly renounced the Annamite costume. She was fluttering about tonight, in a dress cut the French way, vivid red, which fitted tightly around her small waist. This diner was for her like a consecration of her new position: the commissioner offered by this gesture of acceptance an example to all these young, rather derisive Frenchmen, so cynical of the newly weds. She kept herself quite well, this small Annamite, studying the manners of her neighbours in order to eat correctly without the chop-sticks of ivory which was the cutlery of her youth.

Plate 34 *Laotians drinking rice liquor with the aid of bamboo straws.*

After the meal, a temperamental phonograph, that replaced the absent orchestra, played some opera arias in the reception hall. Then it played the first lines of a waltz. All the young people, be it out of courtesy or because they have been weaned from all the distractions of Europe for a long time, invited me with insistence to dance with them. I glided for a long time in this grand hall, realizing that this unexpected entertainment revived for these isolated souls the happy hours of their youth in France: the family reunions, the furtive flirtations with young friends, the sisters in tulle dresses that one accompanied to parties . . . They felt less far away from all that this evening, and less abandoned in this strange country where nostalgia sometimes awaits them.

18 November 1909

Kaé came every morning to take my orders. Today he arrived in such a state of drunkenness that I had to throw him out the door. An hour later, he returned, sobered up and not too ashamed of himself. To the few remarks I made him, he answered by accusing the Laotians: 'They are savages,' he told me contemptuously . . . .'all night, singing, shouting and drinking'—'And have you behaved like them?'—'Yes,' he admitted sincerely. 'You, madam, you were dancing very well last night; I did like madam!'

I was disarmed. He had to pass the night beside a jug full of rice liquor with his happy drinking companions, passing around the hollow bamboo which, in the fashion of our straws, serves to suck out the strong liquor. But to supplement the imperfect services of Kaé, Mr. Grand gave me a little servant from his own house. His name was Bak Soui. He was a boy of some fifteen years of age, proud of his pink *sampot*, supple and graceful as a young girl. Through his care, my room was always full of flowers and all day long he floated around noiselessly in my shadow.

In Buddhist countries, there are numerous locations where legend has it that the Buddha has left his footprint. Luang-Prabang is no exception to this tradition and, there is, in the middle of the city, on a buttress of the Pou Si, a cavity which has more or less the form of a giant foot, to which the Laotians offer their devotion. We will not fail to make this pilgrimage.

Today we are to see the giant footprint of the Buddha by following some prattling women. The road climbed behind the stalls of the market and crossed a monastery with a rather ruined temple. But how charming were the little houses of the monks with their enclosures boasting hibiscus and pomegranate trees. Draped in their canary-yellow robes from which emerged their completely shaven heads, the monks and the little novices were squatting, their eyes vacant, on the verandahs, framed with supply lianas. What were they contemplating in this complete *far niente*, set free from the worries of having to earn a living? At the call of the gong,

73

the locals provided them with their food or the monks walked around to collect their meals in the houses, bringing, instead of the small wooden bowl, a bronze cooking pot which is like a standard attribute from which they never separate themselves. The Buddhist precepts subject the monks to a severe discipline which regulates all their acts and which seems sometimes to derive more from rules of politeness than from religious prescriptions. However, one reproaches the monks of Laos for easily neglecting these laws and, even in this country of light morals, often causing scandal by doing so, if one can believe gossip. Nevertheless, their quiet quarters are far from making one dream of the orgiastic monastery of Thélème![4] In the days of nonchalance, of laziness, of disgust for the useless effort, one would aspire to live like this without thoughts, without wants, almost without moving, in these silent little houses in this flowery garden.

At the exit of the monastery, the ascent became steeper so much so that we have to haul ourselves up with the help of our arms. After half an hour of efforts, which even the belief in God did not sanctify, we reached the top.

Between the shrubs there was a small ruined *that* and the famous imprint—a big hole protected by masonry, around which the *pou sao* squatted immediately upon arrival. What are they doing, so serious, their heads and arms outstretched before them? They meticulously glued, as offerings, minuscule leaves of gold, in this miraculous pit, as they glued them on the statues of Buddha to render this God propitious to their wishes. The sunlight hit a corner of this cavity, it made the precious metal shine and it seemed to light up the entrance to the cave with the treasures of Ali-Baba.

The buttress where we are now, dominates the plain of Luang-Prabang, which is the confluence of three valleys the rivers of which mix their water here with those of the Mekong. Beyond this plain, limiting the view to the North, the mountains once again stack their hilltops of dark greenery, enclosing other narrow valleys of which I will unfortunately never know the wild beauty.

During the descent, we rolled, if I may say so, from the top of a hill down to a street in Luang-Prabang, via a quarter which connects with the front side of the Wat Xieng Thong, one of the most important pagodas of the city. They have nothing greatly interesting to offer, these pagodas, especially if one has seen the ruins of those in Vientiane. Very few sculptures, very few ornaments, recoiled roofs, *thats* in the middle of courtyards, small houses, monks. We entered every-where, to see a caravan of Burmese who are camping here. The pagodas, in effect, offer asylum to foreigners, to travelers, as in the '*Zaouïas*' in Arab countries. They replace hotels. The merchants display their products and sleep, once the night comes, with a ball of cloth under their heads, all under the indulgent eyes of the Buddhas. Nothing among this trash would interest Europeans. We should have met these Burmese when they were on their way to Bangkok, loaded with their elephant tusks, furs, and arms from Burma. Now that they are on their way back to their country, they carry nothing but cotton fabrics from Europe that they have bought in Lower Siam.

Suddenly, a merchant, lying against a wall made a sign to us to approach. With a lot of intrigue, mistrustfully glancing to the side, he uncovered his torso and showed us, introduced under the skin of his arm as a cotton wad, a raw ruby of Siam, big like a pea. He offered to sell it to us but, since the conditions of the sale do not suit us, he placed the ruby immediately back into its hiding place which veils it from the avarice of thieves during long trips . . . .

We have expressed to the king our desire to be acquainted with the queen-mother. She is to receive us this afternoon. Here we are in the court-yard that we have already crossed yesterday, and in front of the royal residence. It's a great Laotian house, divided up by mats of a blinding whiteness, at the door of which the king waits for us. Three royal interpreters are also there, because the queen does not speak French. But, they will not be needed: Sisavong himself wants to interpret.

The queen is a specimen of these old, ape-like women who we have seen so many of in the streets: wrinkles, bones, black uneven teeth in a deformed mouth and a crew-cut of hard, gray hair combed on the head. She is a bit more dressed up than her subjects, her skin is of a clearer yellow, maybe a sign of aristocracy, or the result of long stays in the darkness of the gynœceum. She has nevertheless made the journey by elephant to Bangkok on three occasions when the king of Luang-Prabang went to pay tribute to the king of Siam. She also is very interested in our future journey and becomes enthusiastic when she speaks in praise of the beauty of Bangkok, of which she holds a lively memory.

The kings of Laos have forgotten the road to Siam. We do not meet with princesses loaded with jewelry and dressed in silk in the forest as they went, in

75

curiosity, to the renowned city with a brilliant escort carrying the tribute. The old queen, whose glory has perished, languished in a sedentary way between the king who is not even her son and the little princess that we saw yesterday and of whom she is also not the mother. She came to salute us too, this beautiful, little princess of yesterday, always serious and dignified. The queen-mother is very interested in her and complains because a beautiful elephant which was part of the dowry of the child, had just died. It's a loss of several thousand francs, a very great loss given the total dowry. It's all that we see of the women of the court. Sisavong has not elected a queen yet. His present wives are only concubines of which it is unbecoming to discuss.

In the end, we have seen of the royal residence only the throne room, a long rather cold room, sparsely furnished with armchairs in Chinese style. On the other side of the court, the palace in stone, offered to Sisavong by France, is slowly being built. There is no doubt that it will be more comfortable than this straw hut, although much less amusing for European eyes. At least, it will accommodate the royal family in a sheltered place against the fires, started by malevolence or by carelessness, that often devour the city. Only three years ago, a whole quarter went up in flames without the cause being known. And what an impressive spectacle these fires in Indochinese countries make, when bamboo crackles, and explodes like rifle salvos in the midst of the clear inferno!

After leaving the royal enclosure, the carriage of the *commissariat* led us, along rough roads to the Na Luang, an indigenous farm, some kilometers from the capital. It was for us, an opportunity to see the surroundings. All along the road, domesticated elephants, in the pastures, crushed with their big bodies the hibiscus hedges to make way for us. We crossed a corner of this tropical forest, with its dense vegetation, which is the best thing about Laos and one of its riches. There then was the farm, in a forest clearing with fine and thick herbs. A stream, over which there are rustic bridges, runs in the middle of this immense grassland. Some small horses trotted about freely. Local gardeners were taking water from wells which leant back against the stone houses. Transplanted into Laos, is the setting for a romance in Jean-Jacques' style.[5]

To complete this journey, already well-filled, after dinner, we attended a theater play at the residence of the second king. On the stage, the actors with their frightful or grotesque masks, thrashed about, spurred to brilliance by the bursts of

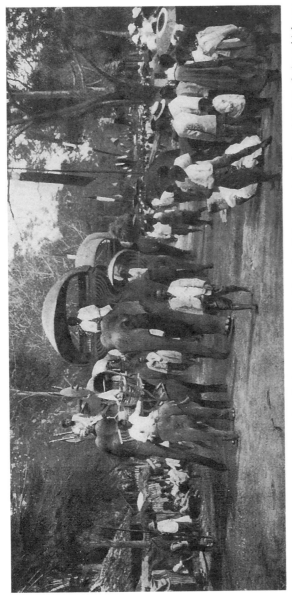

Plate 35 The Royal Retinue: first the elephants approach, driven by their mahouts and carrying two chairs which are facing each other under a large hood.

laughter of the locals who were packed in the courtyard. *Pou bao*, their heads hidden by their covers, *pou sao*, jabbering and lively, exchanged their impressions, giggling with laughter at the funny words, while the babies fell asleep on their mothers' shoulders, like in our popular plays. An orchestra and gongs scanned the dialogue, Chinese lanterns lit up the scene and formed garlands around the courtyard.

It is not necessary to understand Laotian to follow the play. From the movements of the characters, one immediately understands that love takes a prominent role in this play. It concerns, to take away any doubt, savage Othellos, Bartholos held up to ridicule, lovers or conquerors paralyzed by fear, passionate adventurers which are the same in all the countries in the world. We grow weary of the spectacle much earlier than the actors who will, all night, untangle the complicated imbroglio of their comedy in front of the ever attentive spectators.

And everywhere rings out, this night again, the meowing of young lovers in the moon . . . .

19 November 1909

Today, is the great day of festivities. From 8 a.m., in the teeming avenue, a many-hued crowd spreads out and waits patiently for the passage of the king, who, together with an imposing retinue, must leave his palace this morning and proceed to the square of the That Luong. This is because there is also a That Luong in Luang-Prabang, with a pagoda in which the king and the princely dignitaries will exercise their devotions for the festivities of the Laotian New Year. It is a less imposing *that* than the one of Vientiane, but, better preserved, on the top of a small hill which one climbs by a large stone staircase. At the foot of the staircase ia a square, a vast, open terrain around which they have constructed light, little houses for the festivities. They will provide shelter to the king and the princes for two days. The people will sleep in the open, imagining that they are sleeping in the middle of the attractions that the night has in store: theater, dance, fire-works, etc.

Contact with this likable crowd is a real pleasure. Not one false note, not one groan. Everyone smiles, including a group of prisoners who take a stroll while they chat with their guardians, trailing—as the only sign of their imprisonment—

Plate 36 *Monks. Draped in canary yellow dresses from which emerge their completely shaven heads . . . .*

a heavy chain attached to their ankles. By gesturing, I signal to one of them my astonishment that one can in this country of liberty, commit a crime that merits such a punishment. This good-natured prisoner stops me in the middle of the road to tell me a long story under the amused eyes of the onlookers. Does he request protection from me? I do not understand anything of it and tired of trying, he continues his walk looking at me with a big smile.

Suddenly the doors of the royal residence are fully opened. Here is the retinue that proceeds unto the straight avenue, among the trees and the flowers while the standards in lively colors flap in the wind. First the elephants advance, mounted by their mahouts and carrying two chairs, lacquered in red, gold, and fringed with wide trimmings, which face each other under a large hood in silk. Then come the royal guards, in good order, in the same costumes of white kitchen-boys which we saw the day before yesterday, and the grand-officers of the court, the guardians of the precious trinkets of which a king of Laos never separates: teapot, betel box, and a solid golden spittoon.

Finally, dominating his prostrated subjects, Sisavong himself, serious and with dignity under his very high, pointed, tiara brightly shining with gold gilt, the king of the country 'of thousands of elephants and of the white parasol' appears seated on his throne carried by eight servants. Two enormous parasols of white silk, the insignia of his supreme power, elevated at the end of very long shafts, shelter His Majesty. Then banner-carriers and others who balance large painted fans, woven in the form of peacock feathers and of leaves of the coconut tree, throng around the throne.

To isolate the retinue from the crowd, there are two rows of lictors that carry on their shoulders a large saber, with the hilt in the air. From time to time, strange persons seemingly glued to drums shaped like bolsters, beat the ends of their instruments with wooden drumsticks. Their clothes are red and green and they wear little skull caps in these two colors, cut into pointed teeth all around their heads. With their drum-sticks and their funny hats they remind me of the court-jesters of our old kings.

On less elevated and less brilliant thrones, the second, third and fourth kings are carried. They also have parasols but in colored silk. Their sons, their protégés and their servants escort them. After the second king, on a cart pulled by hand, follow

Plate 37 *The* That *of Wat Hate, a pagoda in Luang-Prabang.*

two nice girls, draped and turbaned with gold and silk. Royal princes and high dignitaries, wearing large ribbons around their necks and their hair cut in the fashion of King Yvetot—what a bizarre fashion!—close the procession seated on horses.[6] They precede two horses whose backs are charged with gold and purple covers and with velvet saddles. Respectful ostlers lead these precious mounts by the bridle, while they are fanned with peacock feathers and upon their passing by the front rows of people bow deeper. For whom are these reserved? For no-one . . . . All Laotians know that these sparkling saddles have already been mounted by invisible spirits that have partaken in the ceremonies.

The procession lasts for an hour, very slow, very dignified, without the slightest carnivalesque, in spite of the delight that lies in the eyes, that resounds in the hymns the bursting forth of which dominates the noise of the drums and the gongs. No, this is not a masquerade. It is the celebration of the sun, of gaiety, of pagan elation where every actor has the duty to exercise his vocation and to contribute to the sparkling richness of the whole procession.

Behind the holy horses, the crowd breaks the lines of the two-colored 'court-jesters' and gets underway to the square. Soon the immense square is filled with people. To the 200,000 inhabitants of Luang-Prabang are added the villagers that have come for the festivities. Young people have prepared rockets of fireworks in the villages, i.e., sculpted, armed beams in bamboo of fifteen meters in length, carrying in the interior a tube that shoots forward, also in bamboo. This cumbersome equipment is forced through, with some difficulty to the That Luong where it will be installed for the night celebration.

After lunch, we proceed to the celebrations. Tumblers and comedians are already presenting their acts in the open-air theaters. In the midst of the local people, the Annamite wife of the civil servant, whose acquaintance I made the day before yesterday, is walking her brood of yellow complexioned babies by order of height, holding each other by the hand, all dressed up like French sailors. Cakes and strange fries sizzle on the portable stoves. Upon the arrival of the retinue, Sisavong retired to a room in his hut to shed his heavy royal ornaments and to rest for a few moments. He returned to the overhang, on which the white parasols have been stuck, at 2 p.m.

With the commissioner, we went to salute the king whom we were surprised to find mulching his betel—being a good Laotian. At our approach, he quickly spat it

Plate 38 *Respectful ostlers conduct the horses by their bridles, the velvet saddles of which, according to the Laotians, are possessed by invisible spirits.*

in a high pot, quite the same as an umbrella-stand and I concluded from this that the spittoon in gold was but an ornament on the shelf. Then Sisavong, having become a Westerner again, offered us arm-chairs next to his and invited us to watch the fights between Khas that were to begin shortly in front of the royal residence.

Waists covered by a piece of wool, their long hair falling in strings over their strained faces, the savages clasp each other by the arms. We hear their legs, the muscles of which bulge under their skins, crack. Their ankles seek to trip those of the opponents which would place them at their mercy and, if one of the fighters tires, he rolls unto the hard ground. He does not admit his inferiority, shouting abuses at the winner, to provoke him again.

This spectacle excites the Laotians. In the straw huts of the second and the third king, the high dignitaries bow over, very interested. Around the fighters, the soldiers and the common people squat around in a circle. Others, in order to tower over the spectacle, have taken a seat on the grassy knolls which enclose the square. They have even invaded the staircases of the That Luong and from this crowd a great clamor arises, applauding the winner and exciting the loser.

When the strength of the fighters is exhausted, while the women sponge the sweat from their foreheads and tend to their wounds, large woven baskets are brought to the king, full of areca nuts skillfully filled with a piece of silver, in an act of largesse to the people. The gallant monarch holds the basket for me and invites me to be his replacement in this royal obligation. By fistfuls, I swing the little, green balls over their heads. They flatten noses and blacken eyes. A hundred avid hands are stretched out to receive them before they touch the ground. From the amusing crowd hurrahs, cries of gratitude or appeals ascend: the crowd undulates in large bustles on this immense square. Naturally, I have soon no more nuts while the subjects of Sisavong remain unsatiated.

Night has come. The moon which rises behind the That Luong and behind the paper lanterns which surround the square, only imperfectly lights the agitated crowd. We hear it without seeing it. We guess it is even more densely populated near the royal residence where the dance of the Pou Gnieu Gnia Gnieu, to which the orchestra plays a prelude, will take place. The Pou Gnieu Gnia Gnieu, according to legend, are the ancestors of the Laotians. Their ghosts advance now,

Plate 39 *The open-air theater in Luang-Prabang. Dancers and musicians.*

bizarre monsters, covered with long tawny hairs that hide the lower members. They shake enormous heads and open their immense mouths in a grimace exposing their big teeth. The actors, rigged with cardboard carcasses, proceed with slow steps, shake their hairy members, turn rhythmically, spectacularly lit by a circle of hazy torches. It is like the evocation of some mythological hell.

This dance is followed by the dance of the lamps: the gracious after the grotesque. The dancers roll light cloths around themselves. They strain and relax their supple bodies. They juggle with their lit lanterns which they send flying and the alternating light and dark shadows add mystery to the charm. The musicians beat ever faster with their little hammers on the big instruments with the shrill sounds and the dancers turn about without noticeable fatigue until the first rockets go off and, falling around the That Luong, divert everyone's attention. Then a long clamor rises from the crowd and all proceed to the site of the fireworks.

Later, the theaters attract the locals. We are invited to a special play. The young French of Luang-Prabang have installed a small shadow-play theather in the verandah of the royal residence. They enthrall us with a variety local show: *Do not hit yourself*, in which they have put innocent jests, all their gaiety and the purest French spirit.

Finally, around midnight, the king, reflecting the constraints imposed on him by our presence, offers all of us a grand dinner of Laotian dishes alternating with French. The table is prepared under our very eyes. The table set was well looked after. Even the richest Laotians, who do not have the well ordered menus of the Chinese and the Annamites have never seen it. They also do not use the chopsticks of these other two peoples but eat with a China-cup style spoon with a long hilt, made of porcelain or earthenware. Sisavong has bowed to our customs; we have good, solid silverware and we drink out of superb crystal, especially manufactured for the king of Luang-Prabang in Baccarat.

We are first served Laotian caviar made with the eggs of the *pla buek*—an enormously big fish, the catching of which is only permitted during three days each year for fear of depopulating the Mekong of this succulent species. This catch which takes place in April under the surveillance of dignitaries, designated by the king, forebodes a great celebration—besides, all episodes of Laotian life are underlined by more or less important festivities. Then we eat a *'timbale à la*

Plate 40 *The dance of the* Pho Gnieu Gnia Gnieu.

Sisavong', which contains expensive Laotian vermicelli. The locals are very fond of these pastas and when cooked in the home it provides a pretext for a celebration to which friends and acquaintances are invited. Then there are herbs, leaves candied in oil, the strange taste of which, startles our French constitutions. Luckily, the *foie gras* and European style chicken, of which Mr. Grand's cook has probably supervised the preparation, remind our palates of sensations already well known. They precede the pork, roasted as a whole, the national treat of the Chinese and of the neighboring peoples.

I preside over the meal, facing the king, rather amused by this exhibition of monarchy in which he has made me partake for half a day. But we have to renounce many honors when the hour of leaving approaches, already very late. At night, when we head back to the *commissariat*, we cross the square where the

Plate 41 *The group of elephants at the festivities.*

Plate 42 *The Royal Retinue on its way back to the king's residence.*

celebrations continue until the glimmer of daybreak to end in an orgy, under the protection of the fading moon.

20 November 1909

Last day in Luang-Prabang. I would have liked to utilize the morning to make a pilgrimage to the tomb of the explorer Mouhout, some kilometers from the city, and whom the inhabitants of Luang-Prabang still remember with emotion. In troubled times (1859, the date of the conquest of Cochinchina), he departed from Bangkok across the forest to reach the Mekong in Pakse, the bank of which he followed until Luang-Prabang—a place no other European had yet visited. His notes, collected by a faithful boy, tell—and with what a modesty!—about the boundless energy of this hero of science who went into the adventure without concern for fever or for ferocious animals, classifying plants, collecting interesting insects, only accompanied by some Siamese with whom he shared meals of rice and dried fish. Approaching the end of his journey, he was exhausted by his hardships, undermined by illness and died in a small village on the edge of the Nam Kon, a tributary of the Mekong. Today France reverently maintains his tomb.

Unfortunately, it is impossible today to obtain the men and the horses necessary for this excursion. All the Laotians are exhausted by last night's celebration. Shall I add what is said in a low voice? The long evening, to which we have obliged the king, has held him back from fulfilling his religious duties this morning. At daybreak he was to go to the That Luong to recite prayers, to carry out rituals. However, Sisavong has remained asleep in his hut!

By 2 p.m., the Laotians seem to recover from their numbness. They spread out again in the streets. A great agitation reigns in the square where the retinue prepares for the return of the king. The mahouts run after their escaped elephants which are harnessed. The soldiers and the lictors move the crowd out of the way. The vassals and the servants of each king assemble in front of the respective straw huts of their sovereigns. Thrones and banners are assembled. For one hour, the vivid colors of the uniforms, of the flags, of the lictors merge into each other in a picturesque chaos. Then, the recomposed retinue follows the road returning by the same route between two hedges of prostrated subjects on all fours who start singing one after the other the popular songs of the kingdom, with extraordinary power in their lungs.

Plate 43 *His Majesty Sisavong, the King of Luang-Prabang (Photo Sesmaisons).*

Thus the procession proceeds until they reach the residence of king Sisavong, not without leaving, on the way, the secondary kings with their escorts in front of their houses. But when the big royal doors have closed behind the last guard, the celebration does not continue any less in the streets, without weariness, resembling the preceding days, the hullabaloo of the gongs, the tam-tams, the orchestras that accompany the improvisations of poets and the appeals of love are strewn into the brilliant evening. Ah! what a happy people the Laotians are, loyal to their old customs, to their gracious legends. How they conserve their gaiety in spite of the worst setbacks which mark their history! And how this softness, this naive

Plate 44 *Here and there, strange characters are sleeping on their drums.*

straightforwardness contrasts with the duplicity and the cruel instincts that one reproaches other peoples in the Far East for!

The commotion even invades the house of the commissioner where we spend this last evening, pampered until the end by the delicate attentions of our pleasant host. At midnight, again mingling in the jubilant crowd, we rejoin the cabin of our boat after bidding farewell to our friends of five days, because the *La Grandière* must get started in the early morning.

'Adieu Luang-Prabang! Good-bye Muong Luong,' as the Laotians say. You have intoxicated us with your easy life, with your voluptuous nonchalance, little Capoue asleep between the great stream which guards you and the mountains which extend the odorous shadows of their green dress over you! Good-bye to this awakened dream, to this living tale of fairy queens of which we abandon the magic charm with regret!

21 November 1909

It is impossible to leave at the chosen hour, but, this time the delay is not due to our boys. The Annamite baker of Luang-Prabang who has no doubt participated in the celebration like the Laotians, has fallen short of his promise to supply us with bread for a few days. After several attempts, we succeed only in taking flour with us. Ba will have to improvise as a baker from the first day of the trip through the forest.

We leave the landing at 6 a.m. when the light of the morning already descends from the mountains, sprinkling on the sleeping city a dusty haze of azure and gold. Very fast, the landscape transforms itself. Luang-Prabang disappears after a bend and we are launched on the rapid descend of the Mekong. It's again the savage decorum of the mountains in which the stream is hemmed by steep banks. During the passage, we recognize rocks which we have already met with during the ascent, the loops where we have made calls, but, all this flows before our eyes like the scenes from a cinematograph. Especially in the rapids, we are not only taken by the current but, also by the own speed of the boat which Captain Mélan navigates at full steam to conserve as far as possible the freedom to maneuver in the current. We have the sensation of a descent in a slide, with emotional jolts because the boat leans sideways in a bend of the route or hesitates at the entrance of a channel in a sudden change of speed. Dizziness lies in store for me. I close my eyes . . . . And the engine accompanies, with a mute droning, the growling of a tumultuous stream whose foam inundates our front. The daring maneuver in which one defies danger every instant, wherein one distracted move of the rudder is enough to throw us in the abyss!

Precisely now, in a turning of the Keng Sanioc, the boat suddenly no longer obeys the rudder: it shoots like an arrow towards one of the high sharp ridged rocks which clutters the stream. It's the end of everything, the grinding to pieces in five, four three seconds! We fight the anguish! . . . . The doctor, seated on one of the small make-up tables in the front, has not changed his attitude, caressing his beard involuntarily . . . . I for myself, feel myself turn pale.

During those seconds which were possibly the last of my life, the minute details of the scene, the setting in which it takes place fill my eyes with an ultimate vision, impress themselves, unforgettable, in my brain, and then . . . .and then, Captain Mélan stops us two centimeters from the rock, having been able to throw the engine in reverse even if it means that we are moving to a swallow hole of the rapid. Then the boat which is still not under control inclines, turns in the whirlpool that crushes under us: a danger removed, we fall into another . . . . At last our good *La Grandière* straightens itself, the swallow hollow renounces its prey, the filled depression mends itself further down. I'm returned to calmness again, to hope, to life! Life! It's to Captain Mélan that we owe it, to his energy, to his cold-bloodedness . . . . But he has lost his smile and he is pale from the heavy burden of responsibility. At 4 p.m. we are in Paklay, having made in ten hours the descend which would have taken two days and a half in the ascend.

It's from here that we will leave the route of the Mekong tomorrow to undertake, by horse, the crossing of the forest, the 230 kilometers which separate us from the Menam. The village chief promised us three horses with local saddles: two will be ours, the other will be used alternatingly by Ba and by the cook. He will also obtain for us three packsaddle horses, equipped with the packsaddles resembling those of the European mules, that will carry our cases with supplies and our bivouac gear, reduced to a Picot bed and a Cambodian mattress—because not fearing rain in this season we leave without tents. But, as one cannot charge each of these small horses with more than forty-five kilograms, three packsaddle horses will not be sufficient and we are obliged to take two coolies with us which, unfortunately, will very much slow down the pace of the convoy.

Our negotiations for the organization of this convoy having been accomplished, we return aboard to take a last dinner and spend some hours in the company of our kind comrades who have saved us from all worries, all the material concerns of the journey. They were considerate to our desires, and went out of their way for our convenience. Now, we will have to look after ourselves in an unknown country, in a hostile forest where no-one will wait for us to make a stop-over, where we do not even recognize which are the stop-overs, left to the mercy of a local guide, the language of which, is alien to us.

I have already become a victim to this solitude. I felt disoriented when I ventured alone, in the shadows of Paklay, to find a Chinese shop that could sell us some coffee which the merchants in Luang-Prabang did not have. I found the shop after some difficulty, on the other side of a light bridge across a river, and when I asked for coffee, the Chinese did not understand me, for want of not having Kaé or Ba accompany me. I thoroughly searched myself in their straw hut, shifting a pile of Laotian covers, scattering a cup of areca nuts, stock listing boxes smelling from wicks soaked in coconut oil, but I did not find coffee. I buy tea and a box of sugar: we do without coffee, just like without so many other things.

At night, I return quickly to the river bank. Our baggage has been transported into the little house of the administrator where we will sleep tonight to better facilitate our departure tomorrow morning and also so as not to hinder the early morning departure of the *La Grandière*. A sadness surrounds these last moments together and hovers over the meal in spite of the attempts at gaiety which sound false. The sadness remains with us until we reach our shelter where our co-passengers leave us.

We are alone now, in the small house of the proprietor who has stayed back in Luang-Prabang. Our cases are stacked in a corner of the office. A wax candle dimly lights the nice big bed, with white blankets in which, without doubt, we will sleep little, due to worries related to our departure and also because of the heavy perfume of flowering lianas which cling to the shutters that are open to the forest.

While I re-read my journey notes, the sad news arrives that on 15 July 1910, the unlucky *La Grandière*, descending again from Luang-Prabang to Paklay, met with the fate which it had so providentially escaped during the time we were her

Plate 45 *We met caravans of bullocks.*

passengers in the same area. The conditions were about the same as those that I have just described, but, the outcome tragic rather than emotional. The *La Grandière* has sunk with aboard General de Beylié, the commander of the troops in Cochinchina, and doctor Rouffiandis, the chief of the public health services in Laos aboard the boat. Both of them have died in the catastrophe in addition to two local sailors.

The accident took place in the rapid of Keng Don Soum, not far from Tha Dua. At the moment of the passage the rapid was blocked by an enormously big tree, and avoiding the obstacle, the captain who was then Mr. Mignucci, directed his boat into the too narrow passage still left by the tree. Unfortunately, the *La Grandière* did not obey the rudder (we remember that this had already happened during our journey in the Keng Sanioc rapids) and the strength of the current flung it on the rocks. The captain reversed the engine to free the boat, but, the vessel, being too low in the water was engulfed by a whirlpool seven meters wide, according to a telegram from captain Mignucci. Gripped by the back she sunk in twenty seconds. General Beylié and the doctor were in the front cabin, and did not have time to leave it. In vain one of the locals, hoisted on the spar deck, attempted to grab the general by the hand to pull him up. It was too late! The boat went straight down to a depth of eighty meters and, underwater, the explosion of the boiler completed the task of causing death. Debris from the boat could be found as far as Vientiane, 300 kilometers downstream. The captain, the mechanic, a corporal who accompanied the general and the other locals jumped or were thrown into the water and reached with great trouble a neighboring rock. The *Massic*, a launch of the *Messageries Fluviales* that made a study trip in the rapids of the Upper Mekong, was coming down in the wake of the *La Grandière*. It watched the disaster powerlessly. Arriving at the dangerous passage, the mast of its cabin was torn off by the branches of the tree and the hut was completely swept away. However, it passed through and could pick up the drowning people to convey this terrible news to Vientiane three days later.

The whole colonial press commented on this catastrophe. The tragedy is especially felt in Indochina where General de Beylié, a great enthusiast of Khmer art, was the object of everyone's gratitude for having contributed so forcefully, by his work and personal fortune, to lift the veil that hid the marvels of Angkor. The navigability of the Mekong by steam-boat is again, by this shipwreck, more passionately questioned.

It is certainly true that the *La Grandière* seemed to accomplish a tour de force with each journey and the travels of the *Garcerie* in the Kemmarat rapids gives the same impression. It is also true that steam navigation, while it provides immense advantages for the mail service and for the supply of our posts, has considerably reduced the tribute in human lives that the Europeans paid to the voracity of the stream. If, after this first loss of a steam-boat, one calculates a percentage of drownings in steam-boats and those in pirogues, there is no doubt that this percentage will be to the advantage of the steam-boats. Unfortunately, they are too numerous, i.e. the Frenchmen that have encountered death in pirogues in the rapids of the stream. Every year, for twenty years, some hundred locals and a few Europeans were the victims of similar accidents.

Some recommend the replacement of the *La Grandière* by a boat with a higher bridge in view of the whirlpools and that has a higher speed too (twelve knots instead of nine) in order to more easily dominate the rapids.

The Administration of Laos has for a long time wanted to obtain such a boat for the rapids of Kemmarat. It seems that with a speed of twelve knots, the boat could make journeys during the whole season of the high waters, while now we can only cross the rapids during the medium high waters. Others, in their emotions, propose to abandon all steam navigation between Vientiane and Luang-Prabang. The apostles of this navigation, who have made the first journeys in dangerous conditions of a completely different dimension from those of today, deserve better than a diversion after an initial failure. For a long time to come, the Mekong will remain in this country the only route of communication. Let us hope that the Administration of Laos perseveres, in spite of everything, on the path of progress, replacing in increasing numbers the slow and dangerous pirogues by steam-boats.

Chapter 4

From the Mekong to the Menam Across the Forest, from Paklay to Uttaradit

Our convoy—A Laotian sala—*At the monks—The convoys of bullocks—In pursuit of the tiger—A night under the bamboo's— The forest villages—In a storm—Arrival at Uttaradit—A Siamese governor—Floating houses*

22 November 1909

Early in the morning, a prolonged whistle beckons the departure of the *La Grandière*. She leaves Paklay to redescend the Mekong, while we will take the overland route, across the forest, and join the Menam valley. Soon our small caravan takes to the road.

The difference between the beautiful avenues of Paklay and the road which ewe now take in imperceptible: the same big trees from which lianas with enormous flowers in the form of purple and yellow clocks hang down. This road has been cleared with our passage in mind. By the order of the secondary king of Luang-Prabang, the bamboo bridges across a gushing rivulet which descends foaming towards the Mekong, have been improved.

Our locals precede us. First there are the three conductors of the packsaddle horses who tag their animals behind them. Then, the two porters balance a bamboo luggage rack and a squad of soldiers, provided by the second king to accompany us to the Siamese border. We still have an old Laotian guide, the bearing of a courageous man who instills confidence in me. The naked torsos and even the faces of these locals are covered with blue tattoos that appear also on their thighs, at the bottom of their cotton fabric *sampot*. This *sampot* is fastened to the hip by a leather belt which serves another necessity for the Laotian traveler. They attach their provisions of chewing betel, a bag of rice and especially a big machete, towards which I feel a slightly apprehensive respect.

Plate 46 *Young monks at prayer on the verandah of a monastery (Photo Péri).*

They are delightful our first hours of travel, following our small group, in the inviting forest that draws us to it. We arrived without trouble, by midday, in a rather big village: Muong Wat. Messengers, posted on the road, informed the chief who greeted us, carrying a bunch of hibiscus in an *ô* and the obligatory candles. He conducted us towards a big *sala* (a guesthouse) made of straw, where, well sheltered from the burning sun, we can make a stop of two hours.

We slept at Ban Deum. There is a post of soldiers here and a very small village, the *sala* of which, we occupied. It's quite a strange lodging our shelter for the evening: a plank floor in bamboo elevated on posts to which one climbs by a ladder, a thatch roof and on three sides, as partitions, interwoven branches of trees, adorned with green leaves. It resembled an altar for the Corpus Christi, open to the forest. One clearly smelt the fresh sap because of the still living branches of the partitions, and we were sensitive to the attention of the soldiers, who restored the *sala* for our passage.

Ba bought some eggs and a bony chicken in the village. We will have a real meal. But the bumps of the horse ride have been catastrophic for the cooking pot—some sort of camping oven that we bought in Luang-Prabang which is in pieces—and we are unable to prepare the bread. One of our Laotians possesses a sort of pot in bronze, two fists big, in which he cooks his rice. Ba borrows it from him and the result is that by 9 p.m. he has obtained some sort of heavy paste, burned on the outside and stuck within, with which the old bran balls of the troops would be like brioches.

23 November 1909

Not being able to isolate myself from our local friends, I slept completely dressed last night and was ready from daybreak to pull the chains. By 10 a.m., we found a small shelter of leaves in a forest clearing with a fine carpet of herbs and the soldiers said: 'This is Houa Lat.' We rested until 1 p.m. Then, the ascend amidst the rocks begins. By 3 p.m. we reached the summit of the Pou Dou, the border of French Laos, where the soldiers left us with gracious wishes for a good journey. We keep only the six locals of Paklay and our two servants to enter Siamese Laos.

Having arrived at the summit of the foothills, we now have to follow a trail cut on the flank of a deep valley, which obliges us to ford the deep torrents leading it. At 4 p.m., the assignment of the day is finished. We are on an open plateau, at Muong Tchi Tonne. Twelve huts only, then a monastery and its temple for which we head to find asylum, like all travelers do in this country. But I am a woman, thus of the hostile sex, dangerous. It is not becoming that the monks approach me, neither that they sleep near me. They consent nevertheless to let us install ourselves under the verandah of the monastery.

But, maybe to ward off the evil spells of my presence which menaces them all night, the monks by their prayers, their coming and going, disturb our sleep. They pass by the verandah, carrying little wax candles which dazzle us, descend the ladder, whisper among themselves and go back up mysteriously. Suddenly, the grunting of pigs is heard under our mats. They make me think of the enormously big black pigs, with their huge bellies trailing the ground, that wandered around the monastery when we arrived. Forgetting in my half-sleep that posts isolate us from the ground, I sometimes imagine that I can feel their filthy groans above my face.

24 November 1909

Our packsaddle horses were exhausted yesterday. They were even covered with wounds having been loaded badly by their negligent conductors. Nevertheless, we have to proceed on our travels again. The march today is still quite difficult. Our little horses are admirable. They hoist themselves by abrupt loin thrusts across shaky rocks, they glide, sitting down, with their hind legs folded under them, in descends that are too steep. We let them carry on on their own, trusting their instincts.

All morning, we make the most exhausting march that you can imagine: descending, climbing again, fording across the tributaries of the Nam Pat, a tributary of the Menam which runs at the bottom of the valley. The road passes through the dense bamboo forest that our Laotians cut into with their machete when it bothers us. Sometimes, we have to retreat into the thicket because a caravan of bullocks invade the trail. Every ten to twelve kilometers, we find traces of bivouacs of these convoys: a denuded space, left-overs of fires and beds of bamboo, hanging like hammocks, on which Burmese, big, very dark brown men with ferocious looks and adorned with big turbans, draped with stripped cloths and armed to the teeth like Calabrian bandits, sleep at night. Since yesterday, we have met ten of these caravans each comprising some forty bullocks that placidly march, hitting the obstacles on the road with their charges and wearing around their necks big clocks with wooden clappers, the dry noise of which, signals them from far. In this way, slowly, over an eighteen day period they cover the trajectory, that we hope to cover in seven and a half. Often the trail is buried with their corpses. We found one this morning, still saved from the ferocious beasts: the cow had fallen from exhaustion at the foot of a natural staircase cut into the rocks, each step a height of fifty centimeters, which it had not been able to overcome. These are the caravans that supply Luang-Prabang and, on the return journey, they export the products of North Laos to Bangkok.

Plate 47 *Burmese, installed in a pagoda. They display their merchandise.*

After four hours of this exhausting march, our people and our animals refuse to proceed. We a stop over in a small village, in the shelter of a Burmese hut, close to a river where we make them wash the horses under our very eyes. This is because the Laotians, upon reaching the stop-over, think more of boiling their *nep* (rice) than caring for their animals that simply graze on the leaves of trees. Yesterday, they had forgotten to let the horses drink and they would never have obtained their rations if we would not procure it for them ourselves.

Unfortunately, the village where we are this morning has nothing to offer, neither to us nor our animals, and we can not even obtain from the folk of this country an egg. Savage inhabitants of the great forest which provides for their primitive desires, without any other communication with the world but these short passages of the Burmese; our very presence scares them and they run for fear of our white faces.

Departure at 1 p.m. Still this horrible trail! Hollowed out from the rocks, it is so narrow that it barely permits the riders to pass and it sometimes offers slopes at an incline of sixty percent which our packsaddle horses refuse to climb. Then we have to unload, hoist the horses first, and then, by manpower, the luggage. We ourselves often march to offer rest for our animals, but, the march is very exhausting.

By 5.30 p.m. we are getting worried about this march. The night comes early during this season and it is not wise to travel in the forests after dusk. We know that tigers abscond into the darkness with a man or a horse sometimes without the rest of the caravan noticing it. With Kaé serving as intermediary, we ask our old guide at which hour we will arrive at Naphaï, the closest village which shall be our shelter tonight. He answers: 'At the hour that they put asleep the little children.' That leaves us to know when the Laotian babies are put to sleep! These people ignore watches and dials: during the day, they designate the hours by the position of the sun; at night, their habits provide them with points of reference that serve as indicators.

Finally at 7.30 p.m., the trail widens. Still another stony river to cross and we are in the village. We quickly search for the monastery to ask for shelter. Oh!

Plate 48 *Camp with Burmese (Photo Antonio, Bangkok).*

Surprise, the straw hut is empty. The monks have abandoned it for eight days. They have gone to do a *boun*, some sort of Buddhist celebration, a pilgrimage, in the mountains. I install myself without scruples in their home. We will at last be spared the humidity of the night by a good thatch roof and I sleep under the protection of a series of small Buddhas, that are locked into strange recesses which are adorned with monkeys.

However, our men maintain a torch fire around the monastery because they have fear for the horses. They were informed that last night a panther came to rob the village of its swine.

25 November 1909

Departure at 7 a.m. with a guide obtained by the chief of the village, the guide of our convoy not being sure anymore of the road to follow. The chief comes to kindly salute us while the horses are being charged. His daughters follow him, then other women of the village also approach little by little, dragging their children along. More curious and less wild than those of yesterday morning they want to see the white woman. They have made themselves up, but, do not wear the little trumpets of Luang-Prabang as ear rings, these are replaced by very long metal pendants.

Like yesterday, we first cross the tributaries of the Nam Pat. We even follow the bed of one, a torrent whose more or less dry bottom is covered with rolling stones. The march is quite difficult on these stones and it is really a pity because without them the morning walk would be exquisite. The trench is in the forest. The trees which border these high embankments entwine their branches, mixed with lianas above our heads, in such a way that we find ourselves in a tunnel with archways of greenery where odors of plants and wild saps mingle. Intoxicated with the scents we follow this tunnel in half-obscurity.

Then, at the end of this valley, there is the Nam Pat itself. The capricious trail, using one, then the other bank, obliges us to frequent crossings and even though I stretch my legs as high as possible along the neck of my horse, I get wet up to my knees. But, after this difficult march, we are in a superb forest of bamboos, twenty meters high, clumped tightly packed bundlesand so orderly arranged that they look like they've been planted by some human hand, and since they've been stripped rather high up from their leaves, these bundles give the impression of being enormous trees. Their hollow stems rattle with the blowing of the wind with the strange noise of castanets that solely breaks the silence and the diagonally-ribbed domes, formed by the highest branches, furnish a broad shadow that kills life: no brushwood, the habitual refuge of the animals during the day. Below our feet is clean soil, like a zone with stamped earth. For the first time, I profoundly enjoy, without being distracted by the difficulties of the road, the absolute serenity that fills this solitude.

Further down, the trail becomes stony again, the high bamboo sticks around us cease, replcaed by a horrible glade forest, the stunted trees and the spaces of which possess the aspect of cork-oaks of Provence. The sun burns on us. The last stretch of the morning is very hard under these conditions.

Plate 49 *The coolie porters balancing a bamboo luggage-rack (Photo Péri).*

At 11.30 a.m., we are in Ban Khône and our provisional guide returns to Naphaï. We have but the shelter of a dirty hut during lunch and rest time. The village is miserable. As women and young girls watch us from afar, we search to tame them by holding out lumps of sugar. The temptation is so strong that they approach us trembling. We manage with this bait to obtain some eggs, a delightful supplement to the tasteless canned food.

We leave at 2 p.m. with the intention of arriving for the night at Ban Deun Lek. The forest becomes very beautiful again and we feel that it pulsates with all the beings that breathe from its depths. A band of white monkeys gambles in the highest branches. On the ground, the very fresh marks of a large footprint with strong claws precede us and our old guide points this out to us with a scared gesture: '*Sua*,' he says, which means 'tiger' in Laotian. He moves his hand to his throat to indicated the leap of the animal jumping on a man, taking him to his lair. For two hours we march in the tracks of this fearful friend. On the edge of the

Plate 50 *A camp of coolies under a shelter made of leaves.*

107

torrent that we are about to cross, there are traces of his presence which then disappear to the left: the tiger came to drink at the torrent, then it plunged into the forest again.

The day is waning. We come across the Nam Pat again but, it is so much bigger by the rains that have been late this year, that the old guide wastes precious time to find a passage, and, when he believes he has found one, the night is so dark, the passage so uncertain that it would be careless to use it. We are reduced to bivouac in the forest, in the middle of a circle of big fires to keep away the tiger. The location is beautiful. It's again the high forest with bamboos trembling under the breath of the evening.

Ba, while fixing dinner, prepares in embers his little atrocious breads. We discard some of the empty bottles that hinder us and our local people start a dispute over them as if they were precious objects. Moreover, because we need torches of resin to complete the lighting up of the bivouac, one of the coolies agrees to swim across the river in spite of the darkness, in spite of the strong current and the crocodiles on watch. He is willing to search for these torches in the village that must be a bit farther down on the other bank in exchange for a bottle. For a second bottle, he promises to bring back a chicken from the village. In reality he returns after an hour with the provisions and accompanied by a young boy of Ban Deun Lek who has, no doubt, been attracted by the hope of gaining some bottles.

I stretch myself under my mosquito-net mounted on bamboo sticks. We are surrounded by fire in front of which the Laotians are sitting. They tell long stories in order not to fall asleep all at the same time. From time to time, one of them stands up, throws a bundle of firewood in the blazing inferno so that his silhouette produces a diabolical shadow on the high clumps of bamboo, illuminated by the flames. But, little by little, the cries are but a murmur, the blazes and the torches pale, and fatigue overtakes our guardians. In the silence, the Nam Pat laps softly . . . . Then, suddenly, from the depths of the forest, the cry of a tiger on the prowl shakes me with terror. A neighing responds to it, it comes from the group of our horses left into the darkness some steps away . . . . The tiger—the one of this afternoon or perhaps another—grabs his victim in an iron jaw! . . . . I shout: 'Coolies, coolies, light the fires, *Sua! Sua!*'

Plate 51 *Children in a village in the forest (Photo Péri).*

26 November 1909

Look how dawn bleaches the tops of the bamboo. At the same time, the nightmare of the depressing pitfalls of the darkness fade . . . . A long shudder overtakes the forest. The veil of darkness tears more and more and suddenly there is, in the branches, a cacophony of cries and chants. A wild cock launches first his appeal and others repeat it in the distance. The monkeys—from big gibbons balancing in the branches of the trees on their long, acrobatic arms to the small species that jump in the company of squirrels—grate, cry, whistle, quarrel, like busy pests. The parrots with their flaming feathers clatter their beaks, jabber, pressed as kebab on wobbling bamboo branches . . . . then, the strident criers' nagging falls silent, the sharp concert of little birds starts again, with, to accompany it, the serious cooing of turtledoves.

After having crossed the Nam Pat we leave Ban Deun Lek to the right side without even seeing it, so bushy are the embankments that surround it. At 9.30 a.m. we see a big village, Ban Muong, that we cross quickly even though our people already want to stop in the shadows of a pagoda. We cannot yet consider stopping so early. Two more times, we cross the Nam Pat, so that, like yesterday, we are wet up to the waist on our horses. The men on foot take a complete bath and carry on their heads everything that they usually carry around their belts.

The trail is no longer rocky or mountainous like the first days, but, it's still disagreeable. It's cut through a miry soil and often cluttered with big, fallen trees that our horses find difficulty crossing. From time to time, one of the Laotians turns to the ground and delicately picks up a gilt scarab beetle that shines in a tuft of herbs, and with a dry bite of his teeth he detaches the head which he slurps up without bothering about my disgust. For an hour we followed a great rice-field at the end of which is the big village of Muong Nam Pat. In this village, we find a *sala*. A *sala* so big, so clean, so comfortable, that we cannot resist, just like our local people, the desire to stop here till tomorrow. We will make use of this sojourn to whiten our clothes, and to put the harnessing that needs to be repaired back in order.

Next to our *sala* there are barracks of Siamese soldiers and even a police room which is rather bizarre. It's a large cage with wooden bars. Two prisoners are squatting in it today and they look at us with kindness. The Siamese flag is hoisted to the top of a long pole, erected in the middle of the square. Unfortunately, we do not need to see this red cloth embroidered with a white elephant, flying in the wind, to know that we are no longer in French country: the lack of hospitality of the locals immediately reminds us of it. To all our demands, they answer *'Bo mi'* (there is none), even though pigs, chickens, bananas are swarming around us.

27 November 1909

We leave at 6 a.m. with a young, local boy, our Laotian guide being again uncertain concerning which direction to follow. After three hours of march in a horrible jungle, we re-enter the big forest by running alongside a river, limpid like certain torrents in the Alps. At 11.30 a.m., the guide said: 'Huai Neu.' I do not see a single house, it's only a small clearing at the edge of the river but, the site is delightful. Around the clearing, bamboo, teak, and Indian fig-trees meet, grow old, rot and fall, draped until their death with brilliant coats of lianas, the fresh perfume of which, fights the odors of decomposition that are exhaled by the old stumps. In this part of the forest there are especially beautiful teak trees which are not exploited by lack of means for transportation. Our local people clear with their machetes the area surrounding a gigantic Indian fig-tree. We stretch out under it and it is a delightful rest of two hours in this forest where all beings, hit by the heat, seem to sleep, except for a swarm of diligent humming bees who have made their nest in the hollow trunk of this big tree.

Departure at 1.30 p.m. We tumble back into the jungle, with the sun straight in front of us, covering the trail. An awful afternoon it is, with a heavy heat. We cross once more the Nam Pat, then a small river of the right bank and we find ourselves almost immediately in two villages: La Cane and Nam Kay. So the forest seems to become more populated. But how troublesome is the crossing of a village! Its approach is signaled by a swamp formed by the crisscrossing of foot-trails, trampled and ripped apart by buffaloes in this peat soil. These trails are invaded by young, spiny bamboo-shoots that at the same time enclose the gardens and rip us apart when we pass by. Finally, the villages themselves are so cluttered with detritus that animals alone march on the soil, while inhabitants use walkways made of planks, and fixed to posts, at the height of the huts.

At 4.30 p.m., having left the last village half an hour before, the rain—a strong, tropical rain—surprises us so much the more disagreeably because we have not envisaged the eventuality of such a storm, the season of the rains having long since finished. Our inquiries indicate that Nam Mi, the stop-over for tonight, is still two hours away. We surrender trying to get there in such a down-pour. We have to re-trace in our steps, unfortunately, back to Nam Kay, i.e., make a trip of half an hour, that has been covered already, while the rain pierces us and blinds our horses.

The monastery of Nam Kay offers us a wet verandah, whose rotten floor with holes threatens at every instant to open below us and deposit us in the foul mud, as a refuge. We note sadly upon our arrival that the entire contents of my suitcase are dripping wet. Luckily, in a zinc trunk are the intact clothes of my husband, in which I dress, shedding my clothes that stick to my skin because of the rain. The monks, who use our ladder to enter their home, gaze at us, mocking at our embarrassment without offering, be it well understood, any help. Ba and Kaé request, in vain, eggs and chickens in the village. They come back with four kilos of 'paddy' procured at great pains. Four kilos, for six horses! All night long, I shiver on my bivouac bed which has not been spared by the storm either.

28 November 1909

It is impossible to put on any shoes this morning. The leather shoes that I was wearing, as well as the cloth shoes which were in the suitcase have been soaked by the water and are unusable. I place my feet, only covered with socks, in my stirrups. Still, I am soon obliged to pulls these off since they fall in tatters, torn up by the small, spiny bamboo's on the narrow trail. Then my legs bleed, scratched by the spikes of these damn trees. A beautiful sun, already very hot, blazes in the morning light. During the march, the horses serve as ambulant drying sheds. We suspend to their harnessing in the most picturesque disorder, shoes, mattresses, and clothes.

After an hour, we find Nam Mi which yesterday we had imagined to be farther.

At 10.30 a.m., we see Huai Nam Ton, in the middle of a rice-field. Again this morning, our Laotians wanted to cut short the march. We have to insist that they should not stop here and continue to Nam Phy which we hope to reach at noon. It's an awkward march because of the meeting with two convoys of elephants that frighten our packsaddle horses and throw them with their loads in the brushwood.

Plate 52 *A young Burmese herdsman of bullocks.*

Because horses are very much afraid of elephants, it is impossible to form a mixed convoy of elephants and horses. Unfortunately, at midday sharp, instead of finding Nam Phy, we are surprised, in the midst of spiky bamboos by another storm so violent that we are obliged to stop. This time, the devastation is complete. My clothes which were beginning to dry, spread out on the horses, are again dripping wet and there is no more reserve whatsoever in the zinc trunk. I get down from my horse to search, on bare feet, for an illusory shelter under a big tree. I want to preserve the jacket, that I put on this morning and which is my last piece that is not yet wet. I take it off, place it as a cushion on a fallen trunk and sit on top of it, receiving stoically the shower. At least I can later put on one piece of more or less dry clothing. Our people too were crouching under the branches and we succeeded with trouble to get them to take care of the horses, frightened by the rain and by redoubled blows of thunder. However, the rain stopped a bit, courage! Let's take back to the road in the inundated forest.

We arrived at Nam Phy at 1.30 a.m. We did not have to even consider doing another march this afternoon. Streaming with water, both ourselves and our luggage, at the end of our energy and patience, we were too happy to share with the Siamese soldiers and a Burmese merchant a very bad *sala,* open on four sides. We also had a great hunger, but, also this time we could not count on the local resources. There was no-one in the village. The men were in the rice-fields and the women refused to sell any foodstuff before their return. We could not buy matches and it was only at four o'clock that we managed to obtain a brushwood fire that allowed us to warm up a can of food that we ate with bread, soaked by the rain. We spent the night here. But our night was not a night of rest. We were obliged to stay awake until 2 a.m. to dry our things suspended on bamboo sticks over the fire that we maintained ourselves—the coolies pretended that they were too tired and they refused to stay awake with us.

29 November 1909

This is the last day of our journey overland. We approach the Menam and Uttaradit. We woke at 4.30 a.m. We left Nam Phy during the night, very slowly, because the horses groped along in the pools of mud and the rivers were swollen by the rain of yesterday. When the sun came up, we had finally left the big forest behind us. Before our eyes there was an uncultivated plain, transformed today into a swamp. And also the air had no longer the purity, the freshness of the air of Laos.

We rediscovered, while descending to the Siamese plain, the humid, tropical heat that knocks down all courage.

We had a troublesome march in isolation, to get to Pang Nang Hien, the last stop before Uttaradit, at noon. There was only a small *sala* with a zinc roof which had been invaded by a Burmese caravan with their buffaloes. Without unloading the horses, we made a short stop there. The sun on the bushy swamp made this unhealthy rottenness smoke. But what a marvelous hunting ground, this swamp was! Under our feet, wild cocks and peacocks appeared from every tuft and they took wing in the sun which irradiated their gold and emerald feathers. Unfortunately, it was really too hot to hunt and the riffle would have remained in the luggage had I not insisted on having one of the white squirrels that populate the isolated trees here. We collect the poor little thing, whose long bushy tail colored creamy white, was stained with blood. I would like to conserve the fur, but will I be able to, without formaldehyde to act as a disinfectant. Finally by 4 p.m., at the edge of a sanded rice-field, we were at the border of the Menam which is here a calm river, about a kilometer wide at the most, quite different in appearance, with its blue waters so clear in contrast to its muddy and sinister brother the Mekong.

Alas! This river was deserted with the exception of a shed in which the buffaloes of the caravans are loaded, but, all along the right bank, the houses of Uttaradit press forward against a background of greenery. We had been spotted: barges with flat bottoms approached us and helped us to cross the river with our people and our luggage while the horses escorted us, by swimming across. Then we climbed the embankment which, while being less high than that of the Mekong, is witness to important floods and there we were in a populous street parallel to the river, lined by shops. We felt as isolated as in the forest because nobody waited for us, although the French consulate in Bangkok had informed the governor of Uttaradit of our probable arrival for 29 November. We asked for the *sala*.

We were brought to a poor platform in the breeze which we found totally unworthy of a large center like Uttaradit, but, with which we had to be content provisionally. We spread our blankets like folding screens to isolate ourselves from indiscreet boys who were becoming interested in the presence of foreigners and who climbed the ladder of the platform. Kaé was palavering in a group and suddenly he shouted to us that we were not at all in Muong Uttaradit, but in a suburb, a sort of outskirt, that we had to get back on the horses, to follow the river for another two or three kilometers to arrive in the city itself. I hoisted myself without much courage, emaciated, in my saddle and we left, with an amused escort of boys. The suburb's street was long, very long, and especially it seemed unending to me because of my fatigue and because of the still scorching heat.

At a turn, we noticed a small man, dressed in royal blue silk, shoes, socks, *sampot* and jacket, running towards us. He was very apologetic, smiled and excused himself. It was the governor of Uttaradit, moreover he was a lieutenant-colonel of the Siamese Army. The conversation began rather troublesome with Kaé as the intermediary. It seemed that our arrival was only announced for tomorrow. This explained the abandonment in which we had been left just now. 'But I have already taken care of you,' said the governor, 'your house awaits you. I will take you there myself.'

We followed him. I did not leave my poor, half-dead horse and I realized that my companions offered a distorted version of French elegance to the people of Uttaradit. Our clothes were dirty and torn. The green lining of my toupee of cork sole had run on the white cloth of the exterior. Next to this notable, all glittering

Plate 53 *In the market of Uttaradit there is a chattering and busy life.*

like a Louis XV nobleman who has forgotten his wig, my vagabond-like get-up ashamed me.

Thus we arrived at the edge of the river. There was our house! I noticed then that I had not at all understood the lay-out of this city. It did not look like any other that I had seen so far. Behind the long street which we passed and which consisted of Chinese workshops, there was, on the border of the stream, still another line of houses which, the Siamese inhabited by preference. Strictly speaking, these are not houses, but rather floating huts on rafts, linked to the banks by passageways.

The Siamese are even better friends of the water than other peoples of Indochina. The Menam, which in Siamese Laos is sewn by rapids, has from Uttaradit to the sea, but a very calm course. Consequently, it is much more suitable than the Mekong to serve as a route for penetrating the interior, and it is for this reason that it has long been the only road linking the North of Siam to the capital Bangkok. Naturally, the inhabitants seeking to establish themselves as closely as possible to this road, have found nothing better than to construct houses on rafts. It was in one of these amusing houses that we would live. Partitions made of mats divide it in three sections, further sub-divided as desired by folding screens in bamboo. At the

Plate 54 *There we savoured a delightful rest of two hours in the forest.*

117

front, facing the stream, there was a long verandah made of planks and through which one could see the stream.

This blue water, on which I almost walked, attracted me and I sat down at the edge of the wooden floor of the verandah, my legs bathed in the pure river, without any concern, even for deceitful crocodiles—the Menam is populated by them—that could snap them up in passing. An incredible sense of well-being came over me during this rest in the fresh shade of a light roof, once our destination, Uttaradit, which we had aimed at getting to for the past eight days, had been reached.

Nevertheless my stomach also has its wants. Since 4 a.m. in the morning , we had only had some tea upon our departure, and some sandwiches with liver-paste at Pang Nang Hien.—'Quickly Ba go to the market, there must be a market here. Buy what you want: meat, eggs, fresh fish, fruits, because I want to have a good dinner tonight. Quickly, quickly!' But Ba, he too, was tired. Instead of going to the market, he bought on the bank as close as possible some spoiled fish. It was all that he brought with him together with some pork fat—no fruits, no eggs, no

Plate 55 *On the banks of the Menam: the domesticated elephant takes his share of the family's meal.*

vegetables! I will not have tonight the meal of Lucullus by which I wanted to compensate the privations of eight days in the forest. Let me be well understood, the bivouac beds still served as beds. The Siamese, like the Laotians, as well as the Annamites, sleep without blankets, stretched out on mats. So, tonight, I slept all dressed again. We had to descend farther down, towards Bangkok, to rediscover this precious piece of western furniture: a good bed made up with white sheets. We haven't had one since Paklay.

30 November 1909

This morning, I was a little scared to find our lodgings invaded from the early hours by a group of messy people, with sinister bearings. All the Siamese have these hard, brutal faces. The ones we encountered here shouted a lot, jostled, manipulated harpoons and gaffs. Then I felt my light house glide into the water, jerkily. I suspected some bad trick of hostile locals. However, it was not. Kaé explained to me that the water level had receded last night. Our house was bogged down and the governor had simply given orders to set it afloat again.

Plate 56 *We discover, amidst the greenery, the dome devoid of its gilding, of the Wat (temple) of Phitsanuloke (Photo Antonio, Bangkok).*

119

Then, I went for a walk in the marketplace which was held quite a distance from our house, at the end of the long street that we had followed yesterday. The foodstuffs sold here are the same as in the market in Luang-Prabang. It is incredible all that we can buy in this market for one *att*—hardly two French centimes[1]—in vegetables and local fruits. In the Chinese shops we discovered the strangest assortment of European goods, with mildewed labels. These products bear the names of trading houses of Liverpool or Frankfurt, rarely of French trading houses.

We had brought Ba to serve as interpreter in these shops. However, although he knows the Chinese language used in Canton, he does not understand the dialect used by the Chinese of Siam at all. It is not sufficient to speak Chinese to communicate with all the Chinese. The dialects are so numerous that, from province to province, the inhabitants cannot understand the spoken language among themselves. Only the characters of the writing, keep the same meaning everywhere, and serve the social relations. Since Ba does not read Chinese, he could not be of any help to us.

The two communication lines of Uttaradit, i.e., the stream and the street on the land, are both very animated, but in different ways. On the stream, there is a silent animation of barges that do not, in any way, detract from the serenity of the blue river. In the merchant filled street, there is a prattling and busy life around the shops. Nevertheless, here and there, a large green space, mowed as an English lawn, isolates the public buildings: the army barracks, the post office, etc. . . . . Uttaradit gives the impression of being an important commercial centre. We were very surprised to find it so close to the savage region that we had just crossed through. It will even prosper more when the railway line that is being constructed all along the Menam, to link Bangkok with Chiangmai (Siamese Upper Laos), will reach it. Because the Government of Bangkok, well advised by Europeans, is actively involved in having the railways penetrate all of Siam. While in French Laos we are only at the trial-and-errors stages, the Siamese railways are fully in exploitation and expand every year.

This morning, our brave Laotians left us to return to Paklay. They have kissed our clothes, they have touched their heads to the floor mats of the house and they have put their hands on their hearts in this beautiful gesture of respect which conveys good-bye. Then, I saw them disappear, trailing their horses which limped a bit.

The governor has obtained a vessel for us and the oarsmen, for forty *ticals* (about seventy francs), promised to transport us within three days to Phitsanuloke where we will find a Siamese boat-service to continue the descent of the Menam.

One more night, the gentle house rocks us under the light sway of the whispering waters.

Plate 57 *Buddha amidst the ruins of Ayuthia (Photo Antonio, Bangkok).*

121

Chapter 5

The Descend of the Menam and Bangkok

In a sampan *on the Menam—Phitsanuloke—The Siamese rowboat—Paknam Pho—A Siamese family on a trip—Bangkok, her floating city, her pagodas—A Visit to Ayudthia; the elephant hunt—Sampheeng or the Chinese quarter of Bangkok—On the* Donaï—*The penitentiary of Poulo-Condor—Return to Saigon*

1 December 1909

The boat on which we are going to leave Uttaradit to descend the Menam to Phitsanuloke is at our command. It's a rather big vessel—ten meters long by about four meters wide—arranged in the manner of the small *sampans* of Cochinchina, i.e., the central part is covered with a more or less semicircular roof of bamboo lattice-work. This forms a cradle, 1.50 meters high in its highest part, and in which we are compelled to bend to be able to move around. No windows: two doors, one of which leads to the platform in front were our oarsmen are installed under a flat roof, the other to the rear platform which serves as the kitchen for them. The necessity to leave these two doors open to have air and light, obliged us to live completely under the scrutiny of the Siamese. We felt they were, if not hostile, at least mocking. From time to time, their laughter and their gibes aroused, from above our heads, an echo from a big Siamese woman who, in the kitchen, while supervising the cooking pot containing rice and peeling the vegetables, maneuvered the rudder with a simple push of her toe.

We passed the better part of the day seated near the oarsmen, watching the riverbanks glide by. Villages, bathing in the stream, alternate with fisheries where they sell us an excellent fish with pike meat. Big *sampans*, looking alike ours, crossed or overtook us. The Menam, so clear and so full of people along its cheerfully adorned banks covered with coconut and banana trees, calls to mind less and less the muddy, wild and deserted Upper Mekong. Still the descend of the waters, at present, allows rowing-boats only on this stretch of the river. However, almost all year round, the riverine life is thronged by launches that descend regularly from Uttaradit in a day's time, without problems.

At 4 p.m., the men moored the *sampan* in front of a group of houses and signaled that we would pass the night there. Thrilled to escape from our floating gaol and curious to open up this curtain of trees on the banks, we jumped on the embankment. It's a deception! After some sugar-cane fields, the crops cease. There is only silt and the jungle left. Some clumps of trees emerge here and there. On these trees, in the loneliness of the evening, the turtledoves coo, tender birds that one finds at all latitudes, in all climates, as much as in the oases of the Sahara as in the jungles of Asia. A rifle shot dropped the closest pair to the ground, but, it was impossible for us to locate this small game amidst an undergrowth two meters high and in the midst of which we too had lost our way.

Then we went to the village to try to buy a duck. Alas! The women of the Menam were not more hospitable than those of the forest. Only, instead of the '*bo mi*' which was the usual response of the savages of the Siamese part of Upper Laos, these here they said '*may mi,*' in the dialect of the country this means exactly the same thing: 'There aren't any.' Nevertheless a flotilla of ducks was trampling around in the mud!

2 December 1909

Hardly any incident broke the monotony of the morning. The waters were very low, the oarsmen were so disinterested in our boat and the huge cook had sent so many distracted toe pushes to the rudder, that we were stranded on a mud bank. There were exclamations of the rowers who threw themselves into the water, pushed, pulled at the barge and set her free again after half an hour of effort. When they came back aboard, they were as muddy as the buffaloes in the paddy fields.

By 5 p.m., there was a pleasant surprise, we found a real, very populous, very active city. As far as the eye could see, the houses hugged the border of the river, cut across by launches and hundreds of small boats loaded with people and goods, presented the most diversified spectacle. We were in Phitsanuloke . . . . In two days, seemingly without covering any distance, we had completed the *sampan* journey.

We now had to look for the Siamese launch that would bring us to Paknam Pho, the actual terminal of the railway line that goes all the way to Bangkok. Among all these launches, where is ours? Does she leave tomorrow? We only know that there is a service every two days. Kaé investigated the matter for a long time with the local people, but, he could not translate their answers. Finally, we learned that there are two English medical doctors who live in Phitsanuloke. Let's see them, maybe these Europeans can understand us better. They are very far on the road that follows the stream and on which large buildings in wood, surrounded by lawns—army barracks, the post office, etc.—are bordering. Siamese soldiers ride on this beautiful road with saddle horses. The contrast between the people's life that had remained so primitive and this western life that is seeking to enter with its European style army and its railway line, completed upto here, was striking.

The doctors lived in a pleasant cottage in a big garden. After the introductions were made with much difficulty due to our insufficient knowledge of the English language, we understood that we were with American missionaries of the Anglican Church[1] who had come to preach in Phitsanuloke, armed with diplomas of doctor in medicine which they used to gain the confidence of the locals. They lived here with their wives, blond and gracious Americans, and two beautiful babies. Without understanding what we wanted from them, they spontaneously offered us lodgings and supplies. We refused politely but regretted having done so, because, his shelter would certainly have been much more comfortable than the barge.

There we were, thrown back into the night in search of that Siamese launch about which the Americans had not been able to provide us with precise information. We had to cross the big river in a ferry boat, then we followed the long street on the other bank which is the commercial quarter. Pushed by the busy Chinese, we marched and marched on this unending quay. Finally, there was the very small launch, all black. We reached it, groping around in the dark night which was badly lit by the smoking candle-ends of the barges.

First of all, it was satisfactory to learn that she would leave tomorrow. Kaé discussed the conditions of the passage. The price was minimal, but, there was only one class, everyone was a bridge passenger. Nevertheless, on the upper bridge, I noticed a small cabin, the only one on the boat, and I requested the Siamese captain to let me have the pleasure to use it. Not only did he refuse but he warned me that the use of the upper bridge was prohibited to me since I am a woman. This bridge was reserved for men. I should not, just like the Siamese women, leave the steerage bridge, by fault of which I would irritate the *phys* (the spirits) who, out of vengeance, would sink the boat. This steerage bridge was a closet in front, lower still than the cabin of our barge: it was only one meter high. How can one adapt oneself to this for two days if one does not have the dislocated legs of the yellow women who are accustomed after centuries of atavism to living on all fours! We insisted, we threatened to complain with the governor, the stubborn mule simply retorted: 'The governor governs the city, I govern my boat.' Master next to God . . . . .or better, next to the *phys*, this strange sailor may very well know how to maneuver with a steam-boat, he does not seem more civilized to me than the Laotian of Vientiane who searched for the *phy* that made the *La Grandière* run.

3 December 1909

From the early morning our oarsmen conducted us across the city to embark on the launch. We had seen very little of Phitsanuloke yesterday evening, the night had caught us by surprise too early. This morning though, we discovered in the greenery on the left bank, the dome of a ruined *wat* which had lost its gilt. These cities of the North of Siam possess some memento of an old splendour that they have never regained since the Burmese devastated them (1766) and since the construction of Bangkok has taken away their significance.

The captain generously allotted, in the steerage bridge of the launch, a square of two meters by two for us and our luggage. I had my bivouac bed mounted in it, finding it more convenient to live lying down than to live squatted like the local folk. Blankets, hung up as curtains, helped us once again to isolate ourselves from our neighbors, the Siamese travelers, who piled up on the steerage bridge in an amusing, brightly colored flock of shawls, because, the shawls of Laos are also the fashion in Siam. However, these Siamese women did not wear them around their necks, they rolled them as a belt from the waist to the armpits, leaving their arms and their shoulders naked. Instead of the loincloths, or the Laotian *sine*, they had the *sampot* of the men. On the upper bridge which is forbidden for me, the male passengers were installing themselves. The launch picked them up and dropped them off during numerous stop-overs: peasants going from village to village, traveling monks with their servants who carried the bowl for alms, all brushed against my bed with their feet when they climbed and descended.

The stream was even more animated than above Phitsanuloke. This is because many launches steam up the current, especially launches that trail trains of four, five, six linked *sampans*. Some weeks from now, when the railway line, parallel to the stream, will be opened for business, it will no doubt add to her profit some of this activity.

4 December 1909

The boat set off under a gloomy sky and soon a fine rain started to fall. We were obliged to screen off the steerage deck with canvas so that we did not even have the view of the river as a distraction. The small Siamese women, who no doubt

Plate 58 *In the temples of Bangkok, there are long galleries filled with Buddhas.*

127

were also bored, closely watched us from behind the curtains of covers. From time to time, yellow fingers slid into a slit and unpacked, to investigate our make-up articles: a flask, a hairbrush, a shaver.

We reached Paknam Pho at 5 p.m. There was no mooring bridge. The launch dropped the anchor some distance away from the muddy bank, and it was instantly surrounded by barges that quickly disappeared with the Siamese passengers, without agreeing to take us. Our small companions sailed off cackling, jumping down into the barges splashing about in the mud and in the water up to their knees to reach the bank. One of the fifty barges that were in sight must take us; we saw them palaver without result. During half an hour, we shouted, we showed a silver *tical* which represents ten times the price to bring us ashore, but, these people were too happy to bother about the French in trouble. A barge that had ventured in the vicinity of the launch was taken by surprise as we had jumped in authoritatively compelling its owner to take us down on the bank, a muddy embankment so slippery that you would think you were walking on ice.

The night arrived and the cold rain which soaked our clothes was still falling. Who have we here! . . . . In the darkness we stumbled on a European. It was a German, an engineer of the railways and since we could talk in his language, he helped us out of our problems. We could find at the station, it transpired, a waiting room which we could occupy for the night.

The station was a wooden shack and the room that we were proposed was deplorable! In the corner of the building, the disjointed wooden planks closed badly and the wind and rain blew through it. The only furniture was a nasty pallet, a straw mattress on which some filthy blankets had been thrown. It was written that I would travel all the way to Bangkok without being able to enjoy a bed, without being able to shed my clothes to sleep. After a cold dinner composed of the last of our canned food, we stretched out on straw mattress, shivering of humidity, numbed with cold from the winds that blew through the room, listening to the moaning and creaking of the planks because now it was a real storm that raged outside.

5 December 1909

I left Paknam Pho this morning without regrets. In the clearness of an overcast sky, it did not seem any more welcoming than in the stormy night. Wharves and all sorts of provisional buildings in planks spoiled the landscape. Fuming launches blackened the river. It was the animation without the picturesque character of the end of a railway line filled with scrap heaps.

Happy to let the poor launch continue the descend of the Menam without us, we used the more agreeable and faster railway. This time the bad days were certainly over and in effect, this train, considering it's a train in the Far East, was not devoid of comfort with its cars with corridors and its elastic benches. We would have believed that we were on some small line in France had our travel companions not furnished the local colouring. In our compartment there was the family of a Siamese prince returning to Bangkok after a journey to the cities of the North. Crew cut, gray hair, and with a distinguished and intelligent disposition, the prince wore a jacket cut in European style, but, he also wore a *sampot* of violet silk, black socks and varnished shoes with buckles. The princess had covered her bust with a white, very fine, muslin shirt, adorned with lace, which barely covered her shoulders and her arms, under a blue shawl. Her *sampot* trousers were light blue. Much more than her husband, she had retained the Oriental aspect. First, she was hideous because her lips open in a vile way, fat and drooping, ready to receive the betel shag, and then her manners were surely those of her race, when it got hot at 11 a.m. and she felt the need to take a siesta, she pulled her legs under her, squatted and was, in her sleep, but a small packet of members stacked on the seat. Their son is a chap the size of a French child of eight years of age, dressed like his father, with a bowler hat resting on his ears and earnestly smoking a very big cigar. It seems that in Siam all children smoke.

The train almost continuously followed the stream and stopped in towns bathing in the water—old towns with ruins with the same origins as in Phitsanuloke. These are Lopburi, and especially Ayuthia, the old capital of the kingdom. The countryside was always deserted, except for the immediate edges of the stream which were under rice paddy: The Siamese are too lazy to cultivate this huge valley which is the domain of wild elephants, jungle here, forest there, as far as the horizon which is hemmed in by the mountains of Korat.

At 2 p.m., Bangkok! A real train-station, numerous rickshaws, and some carriages, one of which brings us to a hotel . . . .A quick lunch, installing ourselves in a furnished room of real beds and white blankets, with fine mosquito-nets against especially tiny mosquitoes . . . .and then, do not ask of me any more trials. I wish but one thing: to rest a long time, a long time . . . .

9 December 1909

We have been in Bangkok for four days, waiting for the *Donaï*, a mail-boat from Saigon, which will bring us back to Cochinchina by sea. The waiting here will not be boring. There are too many things that sustain our attention, amuse our eyes in this great city where civilizations mix, where races stumble upon each other, every nation fighting to acquire an overbearing influence on a people who have profited from this struggle to safeguard their independence. It is in this way that it has remained a Buffer State between English India and French Indochina, nevertheless accepting instructors for its soldiers and engineers for its railways from Germany, and liberally welcoming the English, Germans, French and Danish in its public administration. However, it is the English influence which dominates and the English language is the only European language known by the civil servants and the Siamese merchants.

Big business is to a great extent in the hands of the English and the Germans. Regarding retail business, the Chinese are the uncontested masters of it. Very numerous in Bangkok, they have even constructed in the city, on the pattern of the cities in China, a quarter—Sampheeng—in which only they live, but, they have moved to places very far from it. The statistics indicate that there are about 1,500,000 Chinese for 1,700,000 Siamese in Siam. The Chinese smothered the local element with their stores, their shops and stalls, so much so that the whole of Bangkok seems to belong to them. At least, this is the first impression that this city leaves, the one that one acquires almost immediately upon leaving the station and arriving in a wide street, the New Road—never-ending, populous, very poorly maintained, with open sewers and on which an electric tramway also operates. New Road was full of Chinese: Chinese at the entrance of grocery stores, Chinese cobblers, Chinese tailors. It was also the funeral of a Chinese, that obstructed the street with gilt canopy and hired mourners. In reality, there are not only Chinese in New Road, since it is in part of this street and in the sidelanes that adjoin it, that the majority of foreigners of all nationalities have their stores, their churches, their consulates and their banks. But their numbers are too insignificant—there are 2,000 Europeans all over Siam—to change the Chinese character of this street.

Furthermore, not all the quarters in Bangkok are devoted to trade in the way New Road is, and we soon observed, by touring the city, that it offered a variety of appearances.

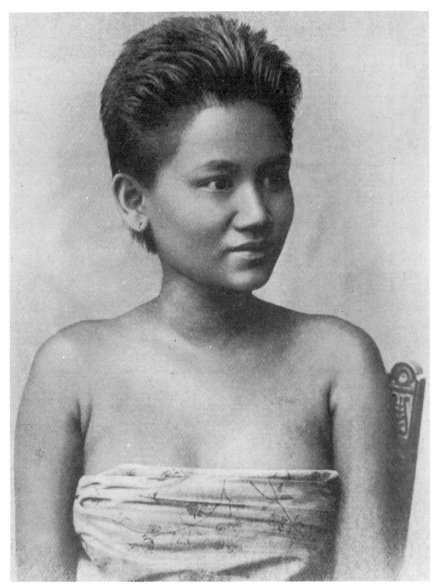

Plate 59 *Siamese woman with the scarf of light silk worn as a belt.*

First the Bangkok of streams and canals. Among these barge loving people, the capital too must have its life's activities on water—the strange characteristic of the cities of Siam. An entire local population lives on the barges which border the large strip of the Menam and on the *sampans* which are attached to its borders. Besides, sinuous canals that cut through the city, are transformed into active streets, like the streets filled with earth, and bordered by floating houses along which barges full of vegetables, grain, and various other supplies move. All the members of a family participate in the maneuvers of these barges: the women and the bigger children hold the oars and the rudder, the small ones stumble on the gangways, paddle with their feet and hands, at each instant risking a dip without even arousing the attention of their mothers. We looked over these animated scenes from the high backs of bridges thrown across these waterways in great numbers, and which cut through the terrestrial streets, having earned Bangkok the name 'Venice of the Far East.'

A discovery trip beyond the city of these canals and the city of the foreigners made us quickly discover the most interesting part of Bangkok, the *royal city*— city of luxury, isolated by a wall from the cesspool of the other quarters. By crossing the gate of this wall with the tramway of New Road, we were struck by the complete change in surroundings. There are sparkling avenues planted with trees and big lawns in public gardens. Almost no trading houses but army barracks, ministries, palaces, a museum, and, on the great square, the Royal Palace, a hotchpotch of monuments with pointed pyres, separated from the royal city by a new fence with towers, gates and crenelations. Inside, there is first the palace *sensu strictu*, the architecture of which brings to mind the Italian style, nevertheless, encumbered by the recoiled roofs, by the pyres in true Siamese taste. There still is a throne hall standing alone, a temple, the treasury, immense outbuildings, without failing to mention the stables where the sacred white elephants are taken care of . . . .it is well known that they are not white at all, but merely a shade of gray which is lighter than that of their brother. An army of servants and Siamese dignitaries with an air of importance, scurried about in the court yards.

But the glory of Bangkok is essentially reflected in the temples, the *wats* many of which are splendid. They defeat the aristocratic royal city with their splendour and they tower victoriously above the leprous decay of the people's quarters. What debauchery of pointed roofs, of domes, of pyramids, of towers, of sculptured, varnished pinnacles laid in with painted ceramic, enamel or gold that blazed in the sun! Every *wat* does not only consist of a temple but of a series of pagodas of all sizes. Then the *thats*, galleries adorned with Buddhas, schools for monks, terraces, court-yards displaying fabulous stone animals, grimacing figures and colossal spirits. And what riches are contained in these pagodas! Without talking about the millions of gilt statues, offerings of the faithful, that lay scattered up to the doorways, every temple prides itself of special splendours. For example, under a teak colonnade Wat Pho harbours a huge reclining Buddha which measures fifty meters in length from the shoulders to the feet. His eyes are of silver, his lips enamel and a layer of pure gold in leaves entirely covers him.

Plate 60 *Fishing in the Menam.*

Nevertheless, the marvel of marvels is the Wat Phra Keo which offers asylum to the small, lively emerald Buddha from Vientiane. This *wat* is constructed within the boundaries of the palace. Nothing has been spared to make it unrivaled, to construct a decorum deserving of this reputed Buddha, the head of which is made of one big emerald. The altars and the incense burners are made of precious stones, jewels and stones are displayed in cases; they sparkle around the necks of statues. In short, the treasures stacked here make of this temple a museum, the richness of which is beyond imagination. I did not experience any similarity with the temple with the same name in Vientiane, while I walk in the Phra Keo of Bangkok. I could not make any comparison at all between the deplorable, overturned ruins in the grass of Laos and these glorious sanctuaries that we are visiting now. If it is true that these are the reproduction of the first, devastated Phra Keo, who would doubt it today?

The oldest monuments of Bangkok are not older than one-hundred and fifty years, since the construction of the city dates from the second half of the eighteenth century. But how much justice does this relatively recent architecture do to the ancient Khmer traditions from which it originates—the amazing Khmer art, born in a powerful empire, the splendid ruins of which Angkor testify to. But since these monuments do not speak for themselves, they have built a pious reduction of the genial Angkor Wat in a *wat* of Bangkok. It is there, the old Khmer temple, displayed like a child's toy on a terrace, and conscientiously reconstructed, not in ruins, as it is today, but as it was in its time of glory, with its palaces, its columns, its monumental staircases. Without doubt, the Siamese architects come to beg from this effigy good inspiration.

10 December 1909

This morning we took the train to Ayuthia, the old capital in ruins which we could not visit during our passage there. With us traveled a French missionary who lives in Ayuthia in the middle of a small colony of catholic Annamites. He made a short stay-over in Bangkok to plead the case of his flock who, it appears, had been molested by the Siamese over an affair involving liquor which we do not quite understand. We gladly accepted the offer that he made us, i.e., to receive us and to guide us through the ruins. Upon descending from the train we followed him towards a landing where some Annamites awaited him with a barge that they adorned with mats and carpets to honor him. One of them, a man from the seminary, took the oars and skillfully sailed through a maze of canals full of barges and floating houses. It is about all that still survives in this fallen city. We were there when the market took place. On the fronts of the floating shophouses were displayed: tropical fruits, vegetables, big fishes and small river-prawns to buyers who bargained while maneuvering their oars. After we had freed ourselves from the many boats, we still required half an hour to arrive at the Annamite Mission: a small church at the edge of the stream and, grouped around it, small houses directly on the ground, calling to mind Cochinchina.

Where did this colony come from? The missionary, with little knowledge of things Siamese, could not tell us. It is possible that it springs from Annamites that

Plate 61 *The countryside is deserted but for the immediate borders of the river.*

have been taken as prisoners of war in the wars that were fought between the two peoples on several occasions.

Father X provided his barge and his people to us to make a first trip to the ruins before lunch. But we were hardly one hundred meters away when our guides started to talk animatedly among themselves while directing their attention to one side of the Mission as they shouted in terror. Then they abruptly returned. Since we protested, the Annamite seminary man who knew some French told us: 'We want to return immediately. The Siamese commissioner has landed at the Mission. He will do bad things to our Father. We want to defend our Father.' This incident was very inconvenient for us. Our program fell through! Furthermore were we really going to end up in the heat of a police operation, in the middle of Siam? It was really like that. The missionary having a discussion with an uniformed Siamese. Soldiers, their arms in their fists, guarded the river bank and we finally guessed the cause of this dispute. The Annamites had committed fraud. In spite of the Siamese laws on the monopoly of alcohol production, they had surreptitiously produced rice liquor and the Siamese had arrived to carry out a search in their homes, to empty the barrels. The missionary protested against the violation of their homes and threatened to complain in Bangkok, but his case seemed rather weak to us.

Finally, the personnel of the fiscal office boarded their boats again. Behind their backs, the Annamites rubbed their hands, they were happy: the Siamese did not find the best hideaway places. Many of the barrels of rice liquor were still full and will continue the delight of our good frauds.

Now it was too late to see the ruins before lunch which was offered to us by the missionary. We hesitated to accept this hospitality but he said goodwilling: 'You will not impose, I have a cook! They have sent me from Bangkok a Siamese nun to take care of me!' He let the nun come. I expected to see a small sister in the dress of France, like the Annamite nuns of Saigon the racial traits of which disappear in the shadow of the veil. It was a good, very Siamese women who presented herself, with an unveiled face and crew-cut hair. Only, instead of the *sampot* and of the light shawl she was dressed in a long, black shirt. The Father explained emphatically that the little one never enters his home, is relegated to the kitchen, and that this is to avoid misleading comments, for which the Siamese are reputed. The cook did not have sufficient supplies: she had not even baked bread.

Rice replaced it. She quickly fried little river fishes, roasted a chicken and we were served by the attentive Annamites who seemed to adore the missionary who had protected their barrels.

Father X joined us in our afternoon walk. We climbed the banks with him. Time and again the remainders of a tower or the broken columns of a temple dominated the jumble of the brushwood and called for our attention. An even greater desolation hung over these ruins, compared to those of Vientiane which they call to mind. This is so because one feels that the ruins of Siam are irremediably condemned to disappear, to the last stone, by lack of pious hands to maintain them. It has been only one hundred and thirty years since the Burmese invaded the country, destroyed Ayuthia and took with them into captivity three-quarters of the inhabitants, while the fugitive king died of misery in the forest. Nevertheless, one would believe that several centuries have gone by since this terrible war so much so that little is left of the monuments of that period. This is because the tropical vegetation is still a more reliable destructive agent than an invasion of barbarians.

We approached the ruins carefully. Our devoted guides, devoted because their protector befriended us, tore up the thorny brushwood to clear a passage, and, when I instinctively crushed the seeds of the jimsonweed between my fingers, the Annamites well acquainted with this poison, used in carrying out revenge among the people of their race, cried out: 'Be careful, madam! The grains make you crazy and kill you.' Another instance of their attentiveness: thinking they would please us, at the foot of a large, dilapidated Buddha they stole some statues, old *ex-voto* objects, so that we could take them along as souvenirs.

The locals roamed around us and Father X was upset by their remarks: 'Do you know what these heathens are saying? They say: 'See, this is a woman for two men.' And his discouraged gesture proved that he had little hope to be understood by the majority of skeptical and sensual Siamese people. He is happy to preach to his small Annamite colony to which he probably has not preached about the following words of the Gospel: *Give to Caesar what belongs to Caesar*, since he closed his eyes to the smuggled goods.

This country of Ayuthia, that is nothing more now than a small city, regains its importance for some days when the elephant hunt is held. It is prohibited in Siam to kill these animals, but, every two years, an immense beat is held to bring the elephants of Siam together in Ayuthia. Hunters, mounted on domesticated elephants, search for wild elephants in the forests and, helped by soldiers, rural police and inhabitants of the valleys they chase the bands of animals in the direction of the old capital, towards a big space, fenced off with big, solid posts that can cordon off the elephants. Closely pressed, the elephants surge into the fenced space through the entrance that has been cut into it. There is such commotion, such an entanglement of bodies, that a dozen animals died this year, suffocated between the entry posts. The king and the court view this round-up from the heights of a protecting stand. A functionary then designates the elephants which he believes are suitable for domestication, they are trained and the others are set free for another two years.

From this instant onwards, the domesticated elephants are responsible for the education of each captive, taking them between them, showing them their tasks, flaying them with their trunks if they appear to be stubborn. One could never overemphasize how astonishing the intelligence of these animals is. Unfortunately, this sensational hunt took place before our arrival. We could only imagine it, while Father X told us about moving stories, at the very location where the final hour of these giants of the jungle had sounded.

11 December 1909

We spent some hours this last day visiting, on the right bank of the stream, some of the oldest pagodas of Bangkok. Seen from the left side, this old quarter looked like the corner of a public park, but, as soon as we set foot on the embankment, we were unpleasantly surprised to find under the shadows but narrow, miry streets— in which the monks dragged their bare feet— and gutters filled with refuse in which fat pigs roamed around. We must cross these gutters on rotting planks to reach the pagodas. These pagodas, more dilapidated than on the other bank, are nevertheless very characteristic by the purity of their architecture. Wat Cheng[2] especially is the most perfect monument of Khmer art that we have seen in Bangkok. We especially admire, in the middle of less prominent pinnacles, a central pyramid, a hundred meters high, on which a steeple in the form of a glittering dome in glazed earthenware is erected. By a hundred and fifty steps we climbed from the foot of this pyramid to a first terrace from where the view showed Bangkok with its many contrasts.

Plate 62 *A Siamese traveling monk with his servant.*

This afternoon we have had another view of the entire city from the heights of Wat Saket, a temple on the left bank, constructed on top of a hill that one ascends by following a gradually inclined garden-path. A monk opened the shutters of a dormer window cut into a big belvedère for us, the whole of Bangkok appeared with its big stream, with the gaps of its canals and its packed greenery which are pierced through by the temples . . . . Around the city is the flat countryside, sewn with rice. In gratitude we offered the helpful monk some money. He first refused: his vow of poverty prohibits him from receiving alms in the form of money. But, since we insisted, he accepted the money, thrown into a fold of his robe, held open, which of course had not made a vow of poverty. An ingenious way to circumvent the problem.

We also visited the International Club of Bangkok, a spacious building constructed in the middle of grasslands in the foreigners' quarter. Behind the house, some Europeans played tennis rather feebly, since the heat, although less suffocating than in Saigon, was not less painful.

12 December 1909

The boat will lift the anchor at 2 p.m., thus I have been able to walk around the whole morning in Bangkok. I visited the Chinese quarter of Sampheeng. I was hoping to discover some old Siamese pottery there, or some curious jewelry, searching the uniformly packed shops along the passageways, that are of one-and-half meters in width and substitute the streets.

For those familiar with Canton, this Sampheeng looks like a corner of the immense commercial city of Southern China, transposed into Siam. The same little streets with tiles, slippery with refuse, the same shop signs made from planks, painted in red or black and covered with gilt characters balancing on the sides of the shops. And in these shops, the same trade as in Canton. Here heaps of vegetables and quarters of cut up pork are stacked on filthy tables. Farther down, a book-shop with its display of old books with characters drawn by a public writer who, big spectacles on his nose, tried his fine brush soaked in Chinese ink while waiting for customers. A barber seated a client on a wooden stool in the same street; he shaved the brows and put shine on the braid. Still in the same street, jewelers chiseled small boxes in massive silver, big bracelets, and belts. Finally, there were the bazaars in which one could find everything: small sandals for the

Chinese, big like the shoes of a doll, a stock of objects made in paper to burn during funeral rites, representing flowers, barges, animals, then boxes of canned food, scent bottles, cheap mirrors, all the hotchpotch objects from Europe in the middle of which, by nosing about a long time, I discovered precious curios of the Far East in jade, in old porcelain and in ivory. Floating in these poorly ventilated corridors and impregnating these leprous walls, an acrid odor of frying oil, of opium and camphor gripped one by the throat.

14 December 1909

The return! First an entire journey of high seas. Then, this morning, at 11 a.m., stopover at Poulo-Condor, the island of the Cochinchinese coast where the condemned locals of Indochina have been imprisoned. It's a mountain with caves within which the penitentiary has been constructed. A sad life for these few French, civilian and military guards, stranded in solitude in such poor company! To the glumness of the place is added the danger of possible revolts and the difficulty in preventing prisoners, ready to try anything to free themselves, from escaping.

This is how in 1904, prisoners serving as employees on the launch of the penitentiary escaped after they had thrown the unfortunate guards into the sea. One has never again heard of the fugitives. It is probable that their small vessel had been unable to resist a storm on the high seas and that they were all killed. Other prisoners of Poulo-Condor, in approximately 1882, tried the same type of escape without having been more fortunate. They went ashore on the coast of Annam which was not yet under our protectorate. But the Annamites, little inclined to provide asylum to these bad subjects, decapitated them and made the fact known to the French governor of Cochinchina by sending back the launch.

15 December 1909

At dawn, we approached the coast and saw again, at the mouth of the Saigon river, the familiar landscape of Cap Saint-Jacques. The pilot came aboard to guide the liner across the meanders of the river. Our journey was approaching its end. There, in the flat swamp, the twin clock-towers of the cathedral were the first to appear from very far, sometimes to the right, sometimes to the left, sometimes in front, according to the capricious twists of the stream. Finally, at 11 a.m. we were moored at the quay of the *Messageries Fluviales*.

Plate 63 *A street of Sampheeng, the Chinese quarter of Bangkok.*

January 1910

I open this journal again to add to it some melancholic news. Poor Ba died this morning. He succumbed to the fevers, to the dysentery, to the exhaustion—consequences of the fatigue of the journey. In vain, I had him treated by French doctors and also by a famous Chinese doctor who heals with medicinal plants and with flour made out of lotus seeds.

Now, because of this death, a heaviness of the heart will be combined with reverie when I evoke the good and the bad days of travel that our poor servant shared with us. Alas! It is to pay too dearly for these sensations, so captivating as they may have been, with the life of a man. Nevertheless, I know that often nostalgic desire will grip me to experience again your big stream of wild angers, your unending forest with the august shadows—oh Laos!—most attractive of the countries of Indochina.

Notes

Chapter 1
The Lower Mekong and the Rapids of Kemmarat

[1] "Me knowed well."
[2] A Renard train is a train with an ordinary engine, capable of running on road surfaces. It was invented by J. C. Renard (1847-1905), a French officer and engineer.
[3] The Idiot and the Pumpkin.
[4] Decauville equipment is used in railways, by the same name, the lines of which have a narrower width. Invented by the French engineer Paul Decauville with the purpose of being easily installed and removed.
[5] Presumably she means with the gorges in France, e.g., in the Provence and the Haute Provence.
[6] Some sort of loose blouse.
[7] Like most animals that do not know the danger of man, nor the effect of being hit by a bullet, the crocodiles are unaware of the danger until it hits them.

Chapter 2
From Vientiane to Luang-Prabang—The Ruins of Vientiane

[1] The name of the vessel literally means: 'in spite of everything.'

Chapter 3
Luang-Prabang

[1] Marthe Bassenne does seem to have this quite wrong, as the reverse seems more obvious.
[2] Tanitus of Egypt is an ancient, Phoenician goddess, an incarnation of Astarte, who was worshipped in Carthago.

143

Notes

³ Probably, Prince Henri d'Orléans was the royal traveler. He is also mentioned in connection with this notable princess in books of other explorers of the time.

⁴ This refers to the creation of the French writer Rabelais. The *'abbaye de Thélème'* is supposedly a place, founded by aristocrats, devoted to hedonism and devoid of social rules.

⁵ Probably the writer Jean-Jacques Rousseau. His work is characterized by a strong belief in excellence of nature, also as a replacement of too rigid a belief in logical explanations.

⁶ The King of Yvetot was an immensely popular song written by French writer Béranger in 1813. The song came out when France, under Napoleon I, was paying dearly for military victories and became weary of glory. The King of Yvetot was put forward against Napoleon's ambitions as a sage. Presumably, Marthe Bassenne has the hairstyle of the time in mind.

Chapter 4
From the Mekong to the Menam—Across the Forest, from Paklay to Uttaradit

¹ One-hundredth of a French franc.

Chapter 5
The Descend of the Menam and Bangkok

¹ Probably Presbyterians.
² Wat Cheng or Chang is now called Wat Arun.